ROBERT W. BLY

PERSUASIVE PRESENTATIONS FOR BUSINESS

SEMINARS • PODCASTS • WEBINARS • INTERVIEWS • MEETINGS

Jere L. Calmes, Publisher
Cover Design: Kaochoy Saeteurn
Composition and Production: MillerWorks

This publication is designed to provide accurate and authoritative information
in regard to the subject matter covered. It is sold with the understanding that the
publisher is not engaged in rendering legal, accounting or other professional services.
If legal advice or other expert assistance is required, the services of a
competent professional person should be sought.

Library of Congress Cataloging-in-Publication Data

Bly, Robert W.
    Persuasive presentations for business / by Robert W. Bly.
       p. cm.
    ISBN-13: 978-1-59918-177-6 (alk. paper)
    ISBN-10: 1-59918-177-0
    1. Business presentations—Handbooks, manuals, etc. I. Title.
HF5718.22.B59 2008   658.4'52—dc22
2008015784

Printed in Canada

11 10 09 08   10 9 8 7 6 5 4 3 2 1

Contents

Contents

Contents

Contents

Acknowledgments

Thanks to my agent, Bob Diforio, for his usual fine work in finding the right home for this book. Thanks also to my editors, Jere Calmes, Courtney Thurman, and Tricia Miller, for making this a much better book than it was when the manuscript first crossed their desks—and for their patience in waiting for it to get there. Finally, I'd like to thank the professionals who taught me how to speak effectively in front of an audience: Rob Gilbert, Paul Karasik, Terry C. Smith, Fred Gleeck, Paul Hartunian, and the late Dottie Walters. Thanks also to Peter Fogel for his tips on speaking at a roast and Gary Blake for his advice on giving training classes, both in Chapter 10.

Dedication

This book is dedicated to
the memory of Helene Cohen,
Naomi Lewis, and Rowena Stecker.

Introduction

Do you enjoy speaking in front of groups? Most of us don't. And many folks find the thought downright frightening.

Author George Plimpton once wrote, "One of life's terrors for the uninitiated is to be asked to make a speech." A survey done by the *London Times* found that more than four out of ten respondents listed "public speaking" as their number one fear. "Today's public speakers can no longer write their own speeches or books, and there's some evidence that they can no longer read them," laments author Gore Vidal. In his book *Speechwriting: The Master Touch* (Stackpole), Joseph J. Kelley Jr. writes: "The word 'speech' sends shivers up and down countless spines."

Fear and loathing of public speaking causes huge numbers of people in all walks of life—from corporate employees making presentations at workplace meetings, to local citizens addressing the town council—to be lousy public speakers. And the inability of employees to articulate is costing corporate America a small fortune.

Speechwriters routinely get paid $3,000 to $5,000 per assignment to ghostwrite short speeches for executives, with staff speechwriters earning up to $100,000 (or more) a year. Professional speakers earn $1,000 to $5,000 and up to talk for 60 minutes, either to educate, motivate, or entertain a group. More than $3 billion a year is spent annually in the U.S. training workers in writing, public speaking, and other basic communication skills. Countless workers are held back in their careers by flubbing interviews for promotions and jobs.

How many times have you decided not to buy something because the salesperson gave a dull or unconvincing presentation? In academia, student evaluations play a bigger role in the decision to award tenure to professors than in years past; a teacher who is boring or difficult to understand will get poor marks from his students. Ph.D. candidates with lousy presentation skills risk flunking their orals. Political candidates lacking in oratory skills often lose elections to opponents who present a better public image and speak more engagingly—think of Nixon vs. Kennedy.

Even though public speaking is routinely cited as one of the average American's greatest fears, the ability to communicate clearly plays a critical role in both business and career success—even in personal relationships. Toastmasters, a national membership organization dedicated to helping people become better public speakers, reports, "Survey after survey shows that presentation skills are crucial to success in the workplace."

Businesspeople today need to communicate clearly and persuasively with customers, co-workers, employees, team members, vendors, business partners, and colleagues—both in writing and orally. Bill Wilson, a speaking coach, estimates that eight billion presentations are given annually in the U.S. alone. Rare is the white-collar employee who is excused from ever having to give a talk or presentation in the workplace.

There are plenty of books that teach old-fashioned oration or are geared toward professional speakers. But *Persuasive Presentations* has a clear and simple goal: To help the *average* person. Whether you are giving a speech before the local Chamber of Commerce or leading a safety training class for factory workers, this book will help you to:

- Become a comfortable and confident speaker.

- Overcome fear of public speaking and get rid of butterflies.

- Gain and hold the audience's attention.

- Communicate your message in a compelling and engaging fashion.

- Get your audience to listen to you and like you.

- Persuade your audience to see your point of view—and take whatever actions you want them to take.

- Impress and satisfy the person who brought you in to speak, so you are asked back for a repeat performance.

- Consistently get evaluations of "excellent" from your audiences whenever you speak.

- Generate leads, sales, new business opportunities, and orders every time you speak in public.

In addition, speakers in every walk of life can find useful instruction and guidance on how to be a better presenter in the pages that follow. This book can help you if you fit in any of the following categories:

- *Businesspeople*—engineers, scientists, professionals, programmers, middle managers, senior executives, support staff, and others in the corporate world required to give presentations in meetings or in front of customers and prospects.

- *Entrepreneurs*—small business owners, self-employed professionals, and other entrepreneurs who want to promote themselves and become established experts in their field.

- *Students*—high school, college, and graduate students making oral presentations or taking oral exams.

- *Educators*—teachers who want to master presentation techniques to become more effective instructors and make more of an impact on their students.

- *Professional speakers*—self-employed professionals who speak part-time as an ancillary profit center, 3,600 of whom are members of the National Speakers Association, and thousands of part-time and full-time speakers who are not.

- *Salespeople*—anybody who spends all or part of his or her time selling products and services.

- *Trainers*—those who want to earn some of the billions of dollars that U.S. corporations spend annually to train their employees in both basic and technical skills.

- And anyone else who has to—either regularly or sporadically—speak in front of groups ranging in size from 3 to 3,000.

I do have a favor to ask. If you've got a tip for your fellow speakers, or you've written a speech that generated a standing ovation, or even better, improved the business operations or changed the lives of the meeting planner or attendees, why not send them to me so I can share them with readers of the next edition? You can reach me at:

Center for Technical Communication
22 E. Quackenbush Avenue
Dumont, NJ 07628
Phone: 201-385-1220
Fax: 201-385-1138
e-mail: rwbly@bly.com
Web: www.bly.com

CHAPTER 1

So You Have to Give a Talk

SPEAKING WELL
IN PUBLIC:
Why it is critical to
your business and
career success

When you are young, you often think you will do great things. You dream of writing a bestseller, starting an internet business and selling it for millions of dollars, playing for the N.Y. Yankees, winning *American Idol*, becoming a high-powered corporate executive with a six- or seven-figure salary, becoming Donald Trump's next apprentice, making a killing in the stock market, or inventing a cure for cancer.

In most of these imagined futures, we see ourselves doing it alone: toiling long hours over a Bunsen burner with beakers and flasks until we shout "Eureka!" and announce our cancer cure. Or hiding away in a garret banging out the Great American Novel on our laptop, for which we are awarded a Pulitzer Prize.

But as we get older, we increasingly realize that virtually all of our significant successes are accomplished with the help of other people—from friends and relatives to clients, customers, co-workers, colleagues, teammates, and bosses. In fact, it is only by delivering extraordinary value to other people that we can convince them to give us the money with which we pay for our lifestyles.

The problem is that when other people are involved, you can no longer do exactly as you wish with impunity. Rather, you must get buy-in from the team. Ordinary team members often can't take action without the approval of a committee. A project leader without the support of the team risks seeing his efforts derailed. Even the boss cannot simply dictate from on high what will be done and when—not if he wants the loyalty, support, and willing cooperation of those in his employ.

For this reason, your ability to communicate with and persuade others is critical to your success in virtually every aspect of your life—at home, in school, on the job, and in the marketplace. If you can't get others to see your point of view, or understand the ideas you want to communicate, your chances of lasting success are greatly diminished.

A radio commercial for a home study vocabulary course correctly points out, "People judge you by the words you use." The ability to write and speak well can help you close more sales, get offered the job you are interviewing for, and convince others that you are smart and successful. "Americans believe that oratorical skill is a legitimate reflection of intellectual acuity and depth of character," writes Bob Katz, a public speaking expert, in an article in *The Record* (2/3/08).

In this book, we show you how to get your ideas across clearly, simply, persuasively, and engagingly in virtually any speaking situation you are likely to encounter today—from an impromptu presentation in front of a small project team to the keynote address at your industry's national conference.

It's a skill that can help you achieve greater success in school, on the job, in your career, and even in your community and home life. What's more, being a confident public speaker can give you greater confidence as a person, making you feel more in command, more competent, and unafraid to speak up for what you want and believe in—whether you're arguing for an increased school budget at a Board of Education meeting or defending the political candidates you support at a dinner party.

Seven Ways You and Your Business Benefit When You Speak

Many people view public speaking as an unwholesome mental chore to be avoided at any cost. For many of us, it's pretty easy to avoid giving talks. As a writer, for instance, I can hide behind my PC and never face a live audience. Engineers and scientists can spend most of their time in the plant or the laboratory, as they were trained to do.

But in life, silence is deadly—or at least damaging. When you fail to speak up as a consumer, you must tolerate bad service and inferior products. Keeping your mouth shut in the workplace can cause an important project to veer off track or even result in liability. Not telling customers and prospects about the breakthrough technology your company has developed can result in their businesses suffering inefficiency and prevent *your* business from being successful and profitable. And as you climb the corporate ladder and assume positions of leadership, you will be expected to communicate your vision and ideas to others.

Whether you love speaking and aspire to be a professional speaker addressing a crowd of thousands, or you hate to speak in front of groups but have to anyway, becoming a confident, comfortable, engaging public speaker can pay big dividends in a number of ways:

1. Speaking at industry events, such as conferences and trade shows, can help position you as an expert or even a guru in your field. When your competitors constantly appear on the programs of major industry meetings instead of you, it gives them the spotlight and puts you at a competitive disadvantage.

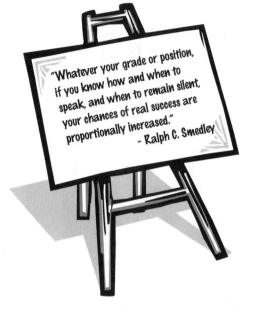

"Whatever your grade or position, if you know how and when to speak, and when to remain silent, your chances of real success are proportionally increased."
— Ralph C. Smedley

2. Giving talks to groups whose members are your prospects can generate awareness of your company, interest in your product, and even direct leads from prospects who want to buy what you are selling. Using techniques I share with you later in this book, you can get anywhere from 50 to 90 percent of the attendees at your event to give you their business cards for follow up.

3. When you prepare a lecture or teach a seminar or class, it requires you to organize your expertise in a clear, logical fashion and to do any research necessary to fill in the gaps in your knowledge. Whenever I agree to teach or speak, I feel I invariably learn as much or more than the attendees listening to me. As a speaker, you don't necessarily know more than other people in your field. But giving talks forces you to organize your information better.

4. When you speak, you usually reach a smaller audience than you would by writing an article for a newspaper or trade journal, or putting up content on your website or blog. But you connect with that small audience on a deeper and more personal level than writing content for offline or online publication. These people convert to qualified leads, customers, and fans at a much greater rate than audiences you reach through means other than in-person speaking.

5. The talks you prepare can be delivered and recycled as useful content in a variety of formats—everything from audio CDs and downloadable MP3 files to podcasts and PDF transcripts. The content of your presentations can also be repurposed for white papers, articles, booklets, special reports, e-books, and other educational and marketing publications. Therefore, you can create the talk once, and then recycle it over and over again, eliminating the need to reinvent the wheel.

Oddly, the same audience often wants to get your content in multiple formats; someone who listens to your tele-seminar often requests the PDF transcript of the same content. The reason is because different people have different primary modes of learning. *The four basic modes of learning are reading, listening, watching, and experiencing.* By repackaging your content and making it available in multiple formats, you can satisfy all four learning modes and reach the widest audience possible.

6. Many of your prospects and students learn more effectively from a talk than from other communications. A live lecture can combine all four of the modes of learning. The audience can read the text on your PowerPoint slides; listen to your voice; watch video clips; view photos, drawings, and graphics; and participate in hands-on exercises. There is really no more effective or impactful way to get your message across than standing in front of a live audience, but that's only true if you are an excellent speaker—something this book will show you how to become.

7. Public speaking generates favorable publicity for your business. All else being equal, those vendors, consultants, and suppliers who speak frequently at workshops, meetings, and seminars have a leg up on their competitors: they get greater exposure and enjoy increased visibility. They are able to deliver their message to influential people at events where these folks go to learn. When you speak, you are viewed as the knowledgeable expert in your field, provided you deliver real value in your talk and not a thinly disguised sales pitch.

Formats and Venues

I'd venture to say that every hour of every working day, there are hundreds of business executives, managers, trainers, teachers, and salespeople giving presentations of some kind all over the world—and there are more variations in venue and audience than we can list here. Chapter 10 reviews specific tips for talks you may be asked to give, but let's take a look here at the major categories of presentations—the ones you are most likely to be asked to speak some day and are dealt with throughout this book:

- *Speeches.* A speech is typically a 20-minute talk delivered from a lectern or podium at an awards ceremony, sales meeting, or other important event. Speeches are one of the more formal modes of presentation. Some speakers read their speeches from a script; others speak from notes or an outline; and some are able to deliver speeches off the cuff. A speech has little or no interaction: you speak and the audience listens. There may be a brief question and answer period. A speech can be serious and somber, light-hearted and humorous, motivational and inspirational, emotional, or persuasive. Political candidates, politicians, senior executives, and association officers are some of the people most likely to deliver speeches.

- *Presentations.* When someone asks you to "make a presentation," it usually means to speak before a group ranging from 3 to 300 or more, typically to convey information and usually using PowerPoint. Length can range from five minutes to an hour or longer. Presentations are more content-driven, while speeches often promote an idea, plan, cause, or point of view.

- *Seminars.* A seminar is a presentation given for educational purposes in a longer format—anywhere from two hours to several days, though most seminars are a half-day or full-day. Seminars can be public or private. In a public seminar, you invite members of the public using newspaper ads, direct mail, or e-mail marketing. Attendees are often, though not always, charged a fee to attend, which can range from $50 to $200 per day or higher. In a private seminar, a corporation pays you to lecture a group of their employees, usually at their offices or in a hotel conference room they arrange and pay for. People attend seminars to gain practical, actionable ideas, not theory. The more real-world experience and stories from the trenches you can share with them, the more involved and engaged your audience.

- *Workshops.* While a seminar is mainly lecture, a workshop implies more attendee participation and interaction. In a business-writing workshop, for instance, the speaker may review and critique writing samples submitted by the attendees, who might also work on writing exercises during the workshop either individually or in small groups. Workshops are the format of choice for skills that are best learned through hands-on experience and practice, such as how to repair an engine or use a spreadsheet.

- *Conferences.* A conference is an event, ranging from one to three days in length, featuring multiple presenters, and typically aimed at either a business audience, hobbyists, or other affinity groups; e.g., RV owners, people who have adopted dogs from shelters, cancer survivors, women who breastfeed their babies, etc. Some speakers address the entire group. Others make their presentations in breakout sessions (see Chapter 10), during which multiple talks are given simultaneously, and the attendees can choose which to attend.

"You will never be a senior account executive unless you learn to make good presentations. Most of your clients will be large corporations, and you must be able to sell plans and campaigns to their committees."
- David Ogilvy

- *Boot camps.* A boot camp is an intensive workshop or seminar, usually held during two or three days, often during a weekend. Attendees pay large registration fees ranging from $977 to $5,000 or more, usually out of their own pockets, to gain a skill or knowledge they believe can transform their lives. Topics can range from finding happiness or true love, to becoming wealthy or starting a small business, to investing in real estate or precious metals. Boot camps usually have multiple speakers, though often the promoter of the event is the main speaker.

- *Training.* Training refers to seminars or workshops designed to teach the attendees specific technical, trade, or workplace skills, or even specific business or company procedures or regulations—for instance, a training session might show plant managers how to comply with OSHA safety regulations. Training sessions are often privately held for companies on site, though public training sessions are available. Depending on the subject, class size can range from half a dozen to two dozen or more students per session. When class size gets much beyond two dozen trainees, the instructor loses the ability to give students a lot of individualized attention or answer all their questions. Training classes can be straight lecture or a combination of lecture and hands-on learning.

- *Briefings.* A briefing may be an *executive briefing* during which a senior executive or department head briefs other executives on important company or business developments, or it can be an *employee briefing* where the rank-and-file is similarly addressed. Briefings are normally given by the executive in charge of the group of listeners. While the senior executive has the authority to require the group to follow his ideas or plans, he knows that projects and initiatives go smoother when the team buys into the idea and has some ownership of it.

- *Workplace meetings.* A workplace meeting is a meeting that takes place in the office and is attended by company employees. Workplace meetings can be impromptu or scheduled, and involve as few as a handful of employees or as many as an entire project team. Topics can range from critical business and technical issues to getting a new vending machine for the lunchroom. The format may simply be a discussion around a conference table, or it may involve short presentations by one or more of the group or team members.

Turning Speaking into a PR Opportunity or Profit Center

Public speaking—giving speeches, lectures, talks, papers, and presentations at public events, industry meetings, conventions, and conferences—is a publicity or public relations (PR) technique that businesses use widely to promote their products or services.

Why is public speaking so effective as a promotional tool? When you speak, you are perceived as the expert. If your talk is good, you immediately establish your credibility with the audience, so that members want you and your company to work with them and solve their problems.

Unlike an article, which is somewhat impersonal, a speech or talk puts you within hand-shaking distance of your audience. In today's fast-paced world where more and more activities are taking place remotely via fax, e-mail, tele-seminars, and webinars, meeting prospects face to face firmly implants an image of you in their minds. If that meeting takes place in an environment where you are singled out as an expert, as is the case when you speak, the impression is that much more effective and powerful.

Speaking is not ideal for every product or marketing situation. If you are trying to mass market a new high-speed color printer on a nationwide basis to all computer users, television commercials and print advertising are likely to be more effective than speaking, which limits the number of people you reach per contact. And the best way to promote your e-commerce website is probably search engine optimization, not giving talks.

On the other hand, a wedding consultant whose market is Manhattan would probably profit immensely from a talk on wedding preparation given to engaged couples at a local church. In his book *Effective Communication of Ideas* (Van Nostrand Reinhold), George Vardaman says speaking should generally be used when:

1. Confidential matters are to be discussed.
2. Warmth and personal qualities are called for.

3. An atmosphere of openness is desired.

4. Strengthening of feelings, attitudes, and beliefs is needed.

5. Exactitude and precision are not required.

6. Decisions must be communicated quickly or important deadlines must be met rapidly.

7. Crucial situations dictate maximum understanding.

8. Added impact is needed to sustain the audience's attention and interest or get them to focus on a topic or issue.

9. Personal authentication of a claim or concept is needed.

10. Social or gregarious needs must be met.

Speaking is also the promotional tool of choice when targeting your PR efforts to a highly specific, narrow vertical market in which many of your best prospects are members of one or more of the major associations or societies in that market. For example, in the widget industry, if you wanted to reach widget buyers, you might run ads or write articles for the large circulation magazines going to all widget people.

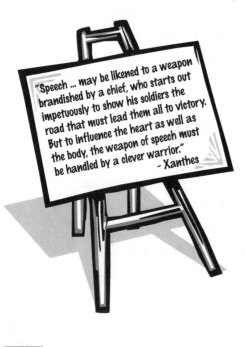

"Speech ... may be likened to a weapon brandished by a chief, who starts out impetuously to show his soldiers the road that must lead them all to victory. But to influence the heart as well as the body, the weapon of speech must be handled by a clever warrior."
                                    - Xanthes

If your company specialized in widget polishing, you might be better off getting known in your field in a variety of ways, including speaking engagements or presentation of papers, at meetings of the Society for Widget Polishers and the National Association for Widget Cleaning and Polishing, if two such organizations existed.

Unless you are sponsoring your own seminar, you will need to find appropriate forums at which your company personnel can be invited to speak. How do you go about it? First, check your mail and the trade publications you read for announcements of industry meetings and conventions. For instance, if you sell furnaces for steel mills and want to promote a new process, you might want to give a paper on your technique at the annual Iron and Steel Exposition.

Some trade journals run preview articles and announcements of major shows, expos, and meetings months before the event. Many trade publications also have columns that announce such meetings on both a national and a local level. Make sure you scan these columns in publications aimed at your target market industries.

You should also receive preview announcements in your e-mail. If you are an advertising manager or the owner of your own small business, professional societies and trade associations will send you direct mail inviting your firm to exhibit at their shows. That's fine, but you have another purpose: to find out whether papers, talks, or seminars are being given at the show and, if so, to get your people on the panels or signed up as speakers. If the show mailing doesn't discuss papers or seminars, call up and ask.

Propose some topics with your company personnel as the speakers. Most conference managers welcome such proposals, because they need speakers. The conference manager or another association executive in charge of the "technical sessions" (the usual name for the presentation of papers or talks) will request an abstract or short 100- to 200-word outline of your talk (a sample seminar description is shown in Appendix III). If others in your company will be giving the talks, work with them to come up with an outline that is enticing enough to generate maximum attendance but also reflects accurately what the speaker wants to talk about.

Because many advertisers will be pitching speakers and presentations at the conference manager, the earlier you do it, the better. Generally, annual meetings and conventions of major associations begin planning eight to twelve months in advance; local groups or local chapters of national organizations generally book speakers three to four months in advance. The earlier you approach them, the more receptive they'll be to your proposal.

You can recycle your talks and give them to different groups in the same year or different years, tailoring them slightly to fit current market conditions, the theme of the meeting, or the group's special interests. When you create a description, outline, or proposal for a talk, keep it on your hard drive. Then, when other speaking opportunities come your way, you can quickly edit the file and print out a customized proposal or abstract that you can fax or mail to the person in charge of that meeting.

Since your goal is to sell your product or service, not educate the audience or become a professional speaker, you want to pick a topic that relates to and helps promote your business but is also of great interest to the group's audience. Importantly, the presentation does not sell you directly, but sells you by positioning you and your company as the expert source of information on the problem your product or service addresses. As such, it must be objective and present how-to advice or useful information; it cannot be a sales or product presentation.

For example, if you sell computer automated telemarketing systems, your talk cannot be a sales pitch for your system. Instead, you could do something such as "How to Choose the Right Computer Automated Telemarketing Software" or "Computer Automated vs. Traditional Telemarketing Systems: Which Is Right for Your Business?" Although you want people to choose your system, your talk should be (mostly) objective and not too obviously slanted in favor of your product; otherwise, you will offend and turn off your audience.

I once spoke at a marketing meeting where one of the other presenters, a manufacturer of such computerized telemarketing systems, was giving a talk. Although he was supposed to talk about how to improve telemarketing results with software, he proceeded to haul in his system and give a demonstration. The comments from attendees were openly hostile and negative. I'm sure he didn't get any business, and this did not enhance his reputation either.

If you are not on an organization's mailing list to receive advance notification of meetings and conventions of your industry associations, subscribe to the organization's e-newsletter on their website. Or call or write a letter. Their names and addresses are listed in *The Encyclopedia of Associations,* published by Gale Research and available in your local library.

"There are three things to aim at in public speaking: First to get into your subject, then to get your subject into you, and lastly, to get your subject into your hearers."

– A.S. Gregg

Where can you speak? Almost anywhere. Clubs, associations, religious organizations, civic organizations, charitable groups, chambers of commerce, community centers—any of these groups might be open to a program that would be both entertaining, informative, and relevant to its members.

You need not be a Zig Ziglar or Tom Peters to succeed as a speaker. A florist can demonstrate the art of flower arranging; a karate instructor can demonstrate the art of self-defense; an art gallery owner can give pointers on buying sculpture; a dentist can talk about saving money on major dental work or how to have a brighter smile.

Make a list of societies and neighborhood groups you belong to, adding the names of local clubs that might be attracted to what you have to say. The next step is to contact the program chairperson and propose your program.

Don't expect to be paid for your efforts. Relatively few speakers are paid. Keep in mind that if you are being paid, you'll probably be restricted from mentioning your own business—no one likes paying for a commercial. As a speaker who is not being paid, you should ask yourself several questions:

- *How many people will attend?* The more people, the more prospects. Make sure that if your speech has visual elements, they can be seen by everyone.

- *What else is on the club's agenda?* As we mentioned, the event may be the incorrect forum for your product or service. You want to speak to people who want to hear what you have to say, not just people who happen to be members and are showing up merely to socialize.

■ *Do you expect to take orders after the speech?* At some gatherings, it is perfectly acceptable for a speaker to hand out promotional information after a speech. However, many organizations feel this is too blatantly commercial, and will forbid you to hand out your sales brochure or even refer to your business directly. Find out how the program chair of the organization you're interested in feels about your blending information with salesmanship.

■ *Remain factual.* Never take a swipe at the competition or indicate that only your product or service can answer people's needs. Good speakers try to remain factual, even when a person requests a comparison between the speaker's service and a competitor's. Try to be a spokesperson for your field, and, in that way, you rise above petty squabbles and are perceived as an authoritative source of information, not just another person with something to sell.

On occasion, meeting planners and conference executives may call and ask you (or a representative from your firm) to speak at their event, rather than you having to seek them out and ask them. This is flattering—but beware. Not every opportunity to speak is really worthwhile. Meeting planners and committee executives are primarily concerned with getting someone to stand at the podium, and do not care whether your speaker or your firm will benefit in any way from the exposure. So, before you say yes to an opportunity to speak, ask the meeting planner the following questions:

■ What is the nature of the group?

■ Who are the members? What are their job titles and responsibilities? What companies do they work for?

■ What is the average attendance of such meetings? How many people does the meeting planner expect will attend your session?

■ Do they pay an honorarium or at least cover expenses?

- What other speakers have they had recently and what firms do these speakers represent?

- Do they pay those other speakers? If so, why not you too?

If the answers indicate that the meeting is not right or worthwhile for your company, or if the meeting planner seems unable or unwilling to provide answers, thank him or her politely and decline the invitation. Since your goal is not to make money as a speaker but to promote your product or service, you can use the group's lack of payment for your talk as leverage in negotiating for concessions—extra things you want them to give you that maximize the promotional value of your talk for your firm.

Here are some things you can ask for. You should get all or at least some of them in addition to the opportunity to address the group:

- Tell the meeting chairperson you would be happy to speak at no charge, provided you receive a list of the members. You can use this list to promote your company via direct mail before as well as after your presentation.

  A pre-talk mailing can let people know about your upcoming talk and be a personal invitation from you to them to come. A post-talk mailing can offer a reprint or audio recording of your presentation to those who missed it.

- At larger conferences and conventions, the conference manager provides attendees with show kits including a variety of materials such as a seminar schedule, passes to luncheons and dinners, maps, tourist sights of interest to out-of-town visitors, and the like. These kits are either mailed in advance or distributed at the show.

  You can tell the conference manager, "I will give the presentation at no charge, but in exchange, we'd like to have you include our company literature in the conference kits mailed to attendees. Is that possible? We will supply as many copies of our literature as you need, of course." If he or she agrees, then you get your promo pieces mailed to hundreds, even thousands, of potential clients at zero mailing cost.

- A speech is an effective way of getting known to a particular audience (the members of the organization and, more specifically, those members who attend your presentation). But as you know, making a permanent impression on a market segment requires a series of contacts, not a single communication.

You can easily transform a one-shot speaking engagement into an ongoing PR campaign targeted to the membership of this particular group. One way, already discussed, is to get the mailing list and do your own mailings, plus have the sponsor include your literature in their mail-out kit.

Another is to get one or more PR placements in the organization's e-newsletter or print magazine. For instance, tell the meeting planner you will supply a series of articles (your press releases and feature articles, recycled for this particular audience) to run in the organization's e-zine before the talk; this makes you known to the audience, which is good PR for your firm but also helps build interest in attending your program.

After your talk, give the editor of the organization's magazine the notes or text of your speech, and encourage him or her to run all or part of it (or a summary) as a post-talk article, so those who could not attend can benefit from the information. Additional articles can also be run as follow-ups after the talk to reinforce your message and provide additional detail to those who want to learn more, or to answer questions or cover issues you didn't have time to cover.

- If the editor will not run a resource box with your website URL with the articles, talk to the meeting planner about getting some free ads for your product or service. For a national organization that charges for ads in its magazine, the value of your free ad space should be approximately twice what your fee would be if you were charging for your talk.

■ The organization will do a program or mailing (or both) with a nice write-up of you and your talk. Usually it prints more than it ends up using, and throws out the extras. Mention that you would be glad to take those extra copies off its hands. Inserting those fliers is a nice touch in your press kits and inquiry fulfillment packages.

■ A professionally done audiotape or video of you giving a seminar can be a great promotional tool and an attention getting supplement to printed brochures, direct mail, and other sales literature. But recording such presentations in a studio can be expensive.

Take Notes:

One way to get an audio or video produced at low cost is to have someone else foot the bill for the taping. If an organization wants you to speak but cannot pay you, and especially if its audience is not a prime market for you, say, "I'll tell you what. Normally I charge $X for such a program. I will do it for you at no charge, provided you can arrange to have it professionally videotaped (or audio recorded, or both) and give me a copy of the master."

If the organization objects to the expense, say, "In exchange, you can copy and distribute the video or audio of my speech to your members, or even sell it to those who attend the meeting or belong to your group or both, and I won't ask for a percentage of the profits. All I want is a master of the recording."

At many major meetings, it is standard practice for sponsoring organizations to audiotape all presentations and offer them for sale at the conference and for one year thereafter in promotional mailings. If you are being taped, tell the sponsor you normally do not allow it but will as long as you get the master. (Also make clear that, while you will allow the sponsor to sell it and will waive any percentage of the profits, the copyright is to be in your name, or at the very least, you both own all rights to the material.)

- If the group is a local chapter of a national organization, ask the meeting chairperson for a list of the other state or local chapters, along with addresses, phone numbers, and the names of the meeting organizers for each of those chapters. Then contact these chapters and offer to give the talk to their members.

- For organizations promoting the event online, they will likely post brief bios, perhaps with head shot photos, of the speakers on their website. Ask that your bio include a hyperlink to your website's URL.

A New Model For Paid Speaking Success

What if you want to become a paid, professional speaker?

The traditional model of paid speaking was to market yourself as a speaker to meeting planners at both associations and corporations. You would send the meeting planner a speaker's kit including a demonstration video of you speaking, your bio, a list of topics you speak on, and outlines of the various talks you give.

Your revenue would come mainly from the speaking fee paid to you for your services by the association or corporate meeting planner. On the surface, when calculated on an hourly rate, the pay for professional speakers seems astronomical. Fran, a friend of mine who is a humorist and motivational speaker, charges a flat fee of $5,000 plus expenses for a one-hour talk. That comes out to $5,000 per hour, more than 800 times the minimum hourly wage. Her fee is paid by the association or corporation sponsoring the event, not the attendees.

But wait a minute. That hourly rate doesn't include the time spent traveling to and from the event. Or time spent researching your audience or your talk. Or time spent writing and practicing your talk, putting together the PowerPoint presentation and handouts, or the considerable time and effort spent selling yourself as a speaker to get the speaking engagement in the first place. For a one-hour speech, the door-to-door time to give the talk, including travel, can be 30 to 48 hours, depending on the location and airline schedules—and even longer for overseas speaking gigs.

Many beginning speakers say they don't mind all that. They look forward to traveling to exotic locations, staying in beautiful resort hotels, and eating gourmet meals at the client's expense. But as experienced speakers know, business travel gets wearisome rather quickly. True, you speak at some beautiful venues, but often, all you see is the highway back and forth between the airport and the hotel. Clients appreciate speakers on expense accounts who are frugal and not lavish; I always fly coach instead of business class and eat dinner at coffee shops. If I am speaking after lunch or dinner, I skip the meal. I suggest you do the same; you do not want to feel weighed down, tired, or full when you speak (and the rubber chicken dinners usually served at these functions are nothing to write home about anyway).

The bottom line is that you are not really making $5,000 an hour or anywhere near it when you add in all the travel and preparation time. Speakers can earn a good living, yes; but only a handful of superstars make a fortune. Most of those are public figures such as President Bill Clinton and Mayor Rudy Giuliani, who are said to command $100,000 or more per speech.

When you are starting out, you may not be able to command such high fees as Fran earns, especially if you are speaking for smaller groups such as local chapters of national associations, bookstores and libraries, the YMCA, and community adult education programs. In these cases, you can get hired by negotiating a deal where you get no guaranteed fee, but instead you and the meeting sponsor split the registration fees collected from attendees. This split of fees ranges from 20 percent for the speaker and 80 percent for the event sponsor, to 50/50. Some of the richest and most successful professional speakers today earn the bulk of their income not from their speaking fees but from sales of their products at events featuring them as speakers. There are both pros and cons to this business model for professional speakers.

The pros are twofold. First, it reduces risk for the event sponsor: they are not out-of-pocket for your fee. When speakers charge large fees, and paid attendance at a meeting is poor, the event sponsor can actually lose money. The second advantage of making your money from product sales is an earnings potential far greater than just a flat fee. Top motivational speakers appearing at large rallies, boot camps, and wealth conferences can earn $10,000 to $100,000 or more from sales of their products.

All kinds of arrangements can be negotiated. For the speaker, the best of both worlds is a large speaking fee plus all or most of the earnings from product sales. On the other end of the spectrum are speaking gigs that pay no fee and only a small percentage of product sales.

That's right: Today many conference promoters not only pay their speakers no fee, but they actually take a percentage of the product sales the speaker makes at their event. The logic is that the conference promoter spends the money to gets buyers into the room, and so should get a cut of the profits. Fee splits are negotiable, but most common is 50 percent of the gross sales for the promoter and 50 percent for the speaker.

The cons of speaking for a percentage of product sales in lieu of a speaker's fee are also twofold. The first drawback is that the speaker is sharing in some of the risk of promoting the event. If you speak for a percentage of product sales, it's disheartening, to say the least, to walk into a conference where you were promised an audience of hundreds to find only ten people in the room. And it does happen; it has happened to me. Keep in mind, too, that not everyone in the room buys products. If there are ten people in attendance and only 10 percent buy, you make just one sale. For a speaker whose product retails for $100, that's $100 gross payment for a speech.

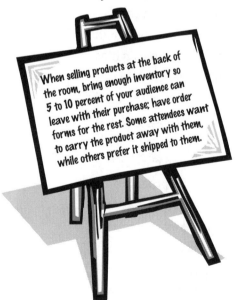

When selling products at the back of the room, bring enough inventory so 5 to 10 percent of your audience can leave with their purchase; have order forms for the rest. Some attendees want to carry the product away with them, while others prefer it shipped to them.

Second, selling products from the platform is an art that takes a lot of practice, one that very few of us are naturally good at. I attended a motivational talk at an advertising convention in the 1980s where the speaker just didn't connect with the group. He was a famous motivational speaker in his day, but his style was old-fashioned and not in any way tailored to our group. Applause was scattered and light, and then the room quietly and quickly emptied out. I remember him standing up on the stage, looking forlornly at copies of the sales flier for his motivational tapes that had been left on the seats and dropped on the floor; I don't think a single person who was in attendance bought his tape program.

If you want to make money as a speaker who sells from the platform, I recommend you read Bret Ridgeway's book *View from the Back* (see Appendix VII), which is packed with instructions on this topic. Bret has been duplicating and fulfilling orders for CDs of my speeches for years, and I can vouch for his expertise and integrity.

Why the World's Top Professional Speakers Aren't Nearly as Good as You Are

Can I be serious? How can I possibly make the claim that you—and remember, I haven't heard you speak—are actually a much better presenter than the world's top professional speakers? It's because today's audiences increasingly value content over style, substance over entertainment, and value over technique. I have seen more professional speakers—many of whom are highly lauded by their peers and industry associations—than I care to remember. In almost every case, it struck me that most of these speakers, especially the ones who billed themselves as motivational, leadership, or sales speakers, all basically gave the same presentation, or at least used these same elements in their talks:

1. They went heavy on the platform technique—voice modulation, dramatic gestures, pauses, and stories. Clearly they were entertainers first and subject matter experts second.

2. Their talks were heavy on emotion and entertainment but light on content, and basically boiled down to some cliché, hackneyed combination of persistence and positive thinking.

3. They often told stories that are not real and not their own, but were lifted from other speakers, usually without acknowledgment.

4. One of their stories usually was real. This was some tragic event in their life that they told in an overly dramatic fashion, often with tears or in a choked voice, designed to gain empathy from the audience.

5. They lightened the mood with one or two humorous stories or jokes, more likely than not also lifted from other sources and unattributed.

6. The objective of their talk was clearly to get rousing applause and a standing ovation from the audience, along with high marks on the evaluation sheet.

So why do I say that you are likely better than all of these highly-trained, dedicated, full-time professional speakers, or will be when you follow the approach to speaking I share with you in this book? It's my observation that audiences have grown weary of the clichéd, cornball "professional speaker," especially those speaking on general topics like motivation, salesmanship, leadership, and success. Why?

In the good old days, there was a scarcity of information, and audiences were looking to be amused, motivated, and entertained by their speakers. In ancient times, going to hear orators speak was a major form of entertainment, along with gladiator combat and plays. Starved for intellectual stimulation, people considered attending lectures a fun way to spend a pleasant afternoon or evening. In the 1800s, one of the most popular public speakers was the scientist Michael Faraday, whose most memorable lecture was titled "The Chemical History of a Candle." Faraday illustrated the chemical principles he covered in his talks with demonstrations, which were often sold out.

Today, we live in an information society, and we are already drowning in content. The speaker is competing with TV, computers, the internet, video games, movies, and many other sources of information and entertainment. A lecture cannot compete with these when it comes to simple amusement. Therefore, today's speaker has to deliver something very specific to engage and win over his audience. In particular, he must deliver valuable and useful content: ideas, strategies, techniques, and methods that solve a pressing problem that members of the audience are facing, or help them live their life better or do their work more effectively.

In the old days, professional speakers were professional orators who had to learn some business basics to give at least the illusion of their talks containing substance. Today's new kind of speaker is primarily a subject matter expert first and a professional orator second. To paraphrase writer and speaker Dan Poynter, we need more talks given by subject matter experts, and fewer talks given by professional speakers. You are a subject matter expert in *something*, and your expertise in your topic is an advantage that few other speakers can match.

This point was driven home to me during a large convention at which I was one of the featured speakers addressing a room of maybe 700 professional and aspiring speakers. The speakers who went before me were polished professionals, trained in the classic mold of a dramatic motivational speaker. Each of them got laughs, applause, and a standing ovation. But I noticed during their talks that virtually no one in the audience was taking notes! Attendees held pens in hand, poised over notepads, ready to write. But the pens were motionless, because the talks were devoid of original content; they had simply heard it a million times before.

When I was introduced, the moderator made clear that I was not a full-time professional speaker, like everyone else there, but was an expert in the subject I had come to teach them: copywriting. During my talk, as I looked out over the room, I saw the group come alive as they furiously scribbled page after page of notes. When I returned to my office the next day, there was an e-mail from one of the speakers who had attended my talk. "You did not have the best platform skills of the four speakers you shared the platform with that morning," he told me candidly. "But the crowd largely agreed that you presented the most useful content; that is, we got the most out of your talk."

In the information age and the internet era, audiences increasingly value substance over style. They are looking to speakers for guidance, wisdom, fresh ideas, and ways improve their lives. They attend talks not for entertainment, but increasingly, for help solving big problems; e.g., how to save enough money to retire or afford college tuition for the kids. You should offer your audiences both expert knowledge of your topic and a clear, engaging presentation style. Both are important. Without the style, you risk boring them, a big sin. But without the substance, you risk wasting their time, an even bigger sin.

It is your speaking ability that gets people to listen and not snooze, daydream, or leave when you are addressing them from the platform. But it is your knowledge, expertise, and experience that get them to come to your talk in the first place. Perhaps you are worried that subject matter mastery is lacking. You need not be concerned. And again, there are two reasons why you should not worry.

First is a principle that my friend, seminar leader Fred Gleeck, teaches that I call the "90/10 rule." Fred says: "It doesn't matter that you are not the world's top expert, or that some others may know more than you. You certainly know more about your topic than 90 percent of the people who hear you speak, and that's the group you're speaking for—and *not* those few experts, the 10 percent, who know more than you do."

Even if some of those experts are in your audience, do not despair. Present a coherent, well-organized, informative talk, and they are likely to praise you for it: what you say will reconfirm what they already know and believe, so they will agree with you, and pronounce you wise.

Second, even if others share fundamental knowledge of your topic, you have had experiences in your field that are unique. Things have happened to you that have not happened to others. Relay those unique experiences and the lessons you learned from them in your talks, and others will value and learn from your successes and failures.

The Number One Secret of Successful Public Speaking

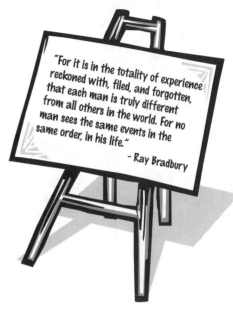

"For it is in the totality of experience reckoned with, filed, and forgotten, that each man is truly different from all others in the world. For no man sees the same events in the same order, in his life."

– Ray Bradbury

In the next few chapters, I'm going to share with you techniques that can help you prepare and deliver a talk that leaves the audience begging for more and makes you shine. But there is one speaking technique I practice that I feel stands out above all others. If you can master this technique, you will be miles ahead of most of the other speakers your attendees hear. It's a speaking method that can help you deliver a superior presentation and overcome your butterflies at the same time.

What's more, this method of public speaking is really simple, and you've already been doing it your whole life. It's called "having a conversation with another person." Let me explain.

You, along with virtually everyone else on the planet, are already an experienced and accomplished speaker. By this, I mean that you speak all the time, every day, almost nonstop—to colleagues, coworkers, customers, supervisors, vendors, suppliers, friends, family, the clerk at the drug store, the waiter at the restaurant—in *one-to-one personal conversations.*

Having these conversations comes naturally. You don't get nervous or scared. And, the people you talk to listen and respond—for the most part. Well, to become a good speaker, all you need to do is have the *same kind of one-to-one conversation with your audience* when speaking in front of a group!

When I am speaking to a group, I look into the audience as I begin talking, find one person who is looking back at me, and make eye contact. Then,

"Be different. No one has loyalty for a 'me too' product, company, person, or service. Be authentic, personal, and consistent. Fakery and wobbling repel fans. Personality cements the bond."
– Marcia Yudkin

I talk to just that one person as if we were having a private, one-on-one conversation. I know everyone else can hear us. But notice: I am not "giving a lecture" or "making a speech," those activities that the average person approaches with fear and trepidation. Instead, I am just having a conversation with one person. "Talk to them as individuals, maintaining eye contact, without a script," advises presentation skills trainer Terry C. Smith.

After 10 to 20 seconds of speaking and looking at one person in the audience, I break eye contact, find another person in the audience, and make eye contact with them. I repeat this process throughout my talk. So I am never staring out into a crowd, seeing an intimidating ocean of bodies. Instead, I am always having a conversation with one person. When you replace the notion of "give a speech" with "have a conversation," you replace formalness with informality, stiffness with warmth, and you make yourself part of the group rather than stand apart.

The result? My fear and anxiety are totally gone. After all, we speak to people every day. Just speak to people in your talks, instead of to a room or a group, one at a time, and you'll be in your comfort zone. Plus, your delivery comes across as much more conversational and natural than a stiff formal lecture or pontificating speech. "Don't write a speech that doesn't sound like you," warns consultant and speaker Mark Amtower. "Write it the way you normally talk: conversational, not professorial. The best speeches sound like conversations and indeed they are." Think about the characteristics of one-on-one conversation, all of which can be used to great effect when speaking to a group from the platform:

- ■ Communication is two-way; you focus not just on what you are saying, but how it is being received by the other person.

■ You make on-the-fly changes in the content and delivery of what you are saying based on your evaluation of how the other person is reacting to it. For example, if you see the person looks puzzled, you slow down and explain it again, making an effort to be even clearer.

■ In most situations, you make a deliberate attempt to come across as a likeable and reasonable human being, realizing that your chances of getting your point across are greater when the other person likes or respects you.

■ You are friendly and natural, not stiff and pompous.

Speaking of sounding stiff, you should never bring your talk written out as a "speech" and read it word for word. Such presentations are unnatural and boring. The listener knows you are reading a speech and thinks, "This speaker could have just e-mailed me his talk to me as a PDF file, and I could have read it at home without bothering to make the trip here!" Instead, outline your talk in bullet form. You can write the bullets on index cards for your eyes only. Or, put the major points on PowerPoint slides and project them in front of the audience so they can follow along with you. But never bring your talk written out as a "speech" and read it word for word.

The bottom line: If you can talk with your kids, your coworkers, your mate, your mom, or your bridge club or bowling buddies, you can talk to a group. Speaking is little more than simply having a conversation with more than one person at a time. In this book, my aim is to turn you into a confident—and competent—speaker. Or if you're already a good speaker, to help you get to the next level. Let's begin!

Speaking and writing on a topic builds your reputation
as a recognized authority in your field.

CHAPTER 2

Planning: The Professional Approach

Understanding Audience Demographics and Psychographics

Just as a computer programmer won't write code until she understands the system requirements, and a builder won't start construction without a blueprint, delivering an effective presentation requires deliberate and careful planning. The planning process for giving a talk includes the steps outlined in this chapter.

Communication requires two parties: you, the speaker or "transmitter," and your audience, the listener or "receiver." Yet one of the most common mistakes I see businesspeople make when they have to give a talk is concentrate on the content and message they want to deliver without considering them in the context of the audience.

"Keep in mind that this talk is not about *you*," says Terry C. Smith, a seminar leader specializing in presentation skills training. "It's about the *audience*. Who are they? What are they interested in? What do you have to give them that will be of benefit? There are three elements in any talk: you, the talk, and the audience. The audience is the most important. Treat them like the VIPs they are."

Even if you are doing all the talking, successful public speaking involves two parties: the speaker and the listener. Of these, I would argue that the listener is by far the more important party. After all, the speech is delivered for the benefit of the audience, not the speaker. If the speaker does not shed light on the topic for the listener, the speaker has failed.

Before I speak at any event, I give the meeting planner a form to fill out and return to me. I call it a Pre-Program Questionnaire (a copy appears in the Appendix II). This questionnaire serves several purposes, the most important of which is to tell me more about my audience in relationship to the topic I am presenting and the lecture I am going to deliver to them.

The first thing my questionnaire asks the meeting planner, aside from the topic she wants me to speak on, is the basic demographics of the audience members: their average age, ratio of male to female, education level, approximate annual income, average number of years with the association or company, and job title and function.

All of this information guides you in tailoring your talk to the audience. The least effective speakers give the same canned speech to everyone, regardless of who is in the audience. Such canned presentations are rarely relevant to the listeners and often poorly received. The more you can customize your presentation to the needs, wants, cares, concerns, desires, and problems faced by your audience, the more meaningful, useful, and relevant your talk will be to them.

Even more important to me than audience demographics, I next ask: "How well educated is the audi-

"A man cannot speak but he judges himself. With his will or against his will he draws his portrait to the eye of his companions by every word. Every opinion reacts on him who utters it."
- Ralph Waldo Emerson

ence in the topic of the seminar?" Knowing this is critical to tailoring your content and presentation to the appropriate level. If you present a program for beginners to experts, your evaluations will be terrible: attendees will be turned off, bored, and insulted. Conversely, an audience of neophytes will be puzzled, confused, and lost if you skip the basics and cover complex technical topics.

Almost as important to me is the *attitude of the audience* as it relates to my upcoming presentation. When attendees sign up for your seminar voluntarily and pay out of their own pocket, they are usually highly motivated to learn. Presentations in which attendance is voluntary, people register themselves, and pay their own way are the easiest to give.

A more difficult situation is in the corporate setting where supervisors and managers require their employees to attend a seminar, especially on a subject in which they aren't interested. A good example is the main corporate seminar I teach, Effective Technical Writing. My attendees are primarily engineers, not technical writers. Most engineers don't care about writing, and the topic does not interest them. They are almost always sent to my class because their boss thinks they write poorly and wants them to improve. They, on the other hand, either think their writing is fine or don't agree that writing is important.

In my Effective Technical Writing class, I start my presentation by asking the class three questions. First, I ask how many of the attendees are there voluntarily vs. how many were forced to go. When I say, "How many were sent here against your will?" it gets a laugh, and all hands in the room go up. Next I ask how many of the attendees think writing is important. Almost no hands go up, and I see the students exchanging glances; they know they are denigrating my subject, and are vaguely embarrassed or uncomfortable about telling this to the teacher. Then I ask the group how many of them are looking forward to the class. A few hands go up out of politeness, but not many. I then say: "Okay. You were forced to be here, you don't think writing is important, and you aren't interested in the class I'm about to teach. Well, wouldn't you really love to be me right about now?" The class bursts into sympathetic, good-natured laughter, and I know I have them in the palm of my hand.

By acknowledging the audience's feelings and attitudes, I win them over to my side and create empathy. They think, "Hey, here's a guy who finally gets me. I think this class may not be so bad after all, so I'll be cooperative with him and maybe I'll learn something." This is in sharp contrast to so many other trainers and speakers they hear who act as if what they are saying is the most important thing in the universe, even though to the trainees, clearly it is not. The trainees resent them, and no bond is established. And here's the thing: It's much easier to teach adults when the audience likes you and respects you, and when they think you understand them and respect them. The openings to all my talks, and we'll discuss this more later in the book, are designed primarily to forge an immediate bond between the audience and me.

Let me give you another example of putting the audience first. I have a B.S. in chemical engineering. Years ago, I was asked to speak at a conference of seniors in college who were majoring in chemical engineering. The speakers on the panel were to speak about their careers. Many worked either as engineers while others had risen through the ranks to become managers. A couple of us had careers completely different than our college major; one guy was in finance, and I was a writer.

As the first few panelists spoke, I could feel the energy in the room draining. The students fidgeted in their seats, and looked bored. It was like bringing your dad into high school to tell your class about your career. The speakers just told their stories, most of which seemed disconnected from the students' lives. They were all about the speaker, and not about the students.

I decided on the spot to take a different tack. I walked to the podium, looked out over the hundreds of students in the audience, and asked: "How many of you want to be successful?" Of course, every hand in the room shot up. That beginning alone was an improvement over the previous speakers, and a tip for you: Any time you can get the audience actively involved, especially doing something physical, even if just raising a hand to answer your question, it instantly engages them. (We will cover more methods for doing this later in the book.)

Then I asked: "Who in the audience can give me a coherent definition of success?" Every hand went down, and none was raised up again. I said, "Everyone in the room wants to be successful. Yet not a single person in the room can define success. If you don't know what it means to be successful, how will you ever get there?" The students were sitting up straight and paying rapt attention. I then gave an off-the-cuff talk on a topic I've written on before, one that I know is on the mind of every college senior: How to succeed in life. The basic premise was that everyone has to define success for themselves, and if you meet those requirements, than you are successful; it doesn't matter what other people say, do, or think. For a group of people about to go out into the world and find their way, the message was relevant and resonated strongly with them.

Know Your Audience on a Deeper Level: Using the BDF formula

To reach your audience on a deeper level, especially in presentations of a persuasive nature—where your goal is to get attendees to buy a product, implement a technology, change a business practice, or alter an attitude or belief—you must understand what bestselling business author Michael Masterson calls the attendees' "Core Buying Complex." These are the emotions, attitudes, and aspirations that drive them, as represented by the formula BDF: beliefs, desires, and feelings.

First, what does your audience believe? What is their attitude toward your proposition, your subject, and the problems or issues it addresses? For instance, if you are a financial planner addressing a group of coin collectors (based on the notion that they have money and are therefore good potential clients for your financial planning services), doing some research will reveal to you that the average coin collector is politically conservative, patriotic, and

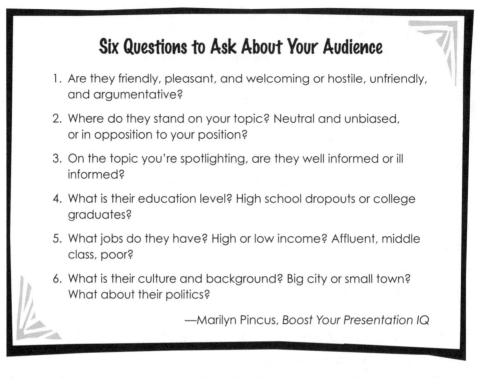

Six Questions to Ask About Your Audience

1. Are they friendly, pleasant, and welcoming or hostile, unfriendly, and argumentative?

2. Where do they stand on your topic? Neutral and unbiased, or in opposition to your position?

3. On the topic you're spotlighting, are they well informed or ill informed?

4. What is their education level? High school dropouts or college graduates?

5. What jobs do they have? High or low income? Affluent, middle class, poor?

6. What is their culture and background? Big city or small town? What about their politics?

—Marilyn Pincus, *Boost Your Presentation IQ*

distrusts big government; many hoard gold coins as a hedge against inflation and a falling dollar.

Second, what emotions are invested in thinking about your topic? How do audience members feel? Are they confident and brash? Nervous and fearful? What do they feel about the issues in their lives, businesses, or industries? Years ago, I spoke to a group of distributors for a large appliance manufacturer. When I asked the meeting planner, a manager working for the manufacturer, what the emotional "hot button" of the group was, he replied without hesitation: "They are afraid they, as the middlemen, are being cut out of the distribution channel as more and more manufacturers sell directly to plumbers and home builders through stores and online." He then told me it was a valid fear, and my talk should focus on how they can survive and remain profitable in such a marketplace.

Third, what are the desires of the audience members? What do they want? What are their goals, hopes, dreams, and aspirations? What change do they want in their lives that your product can help them achieve? For the appliance distributors, the goal was to keep a family tradition alive (most of the attendees were second generation owners) so they could pass a profitable small business on to children.

Another example: We did a BDF analysis using IT people as the prospect group for a company that gives seminars in communication and interpersonal skills for IT professionals. Here's what we came up with in a group meeting:

- *Beliefs*: IT people think they are smarter than other people, technology is the most important thing in the world, users are stupid, and management doesn't appreciate them enough.

- *Desires:* IT people want to be appreciated and recognized. They prefer to deal with computers and avoid people whenever possible, and they want bigger budgets.

- *Feelings:* IT people often have an adversarial relationship with management and users, both of whom they service. They feel others dislike them, look down upon them, and do not understand what they do.

Based on this analysis, particularly the feelings, the company created a promotion that was its most successful ever to promote a seminar titled "Interpersonal Skills for IT Professionals." The headline: "Important news for any IT professional who has ever felt like telling an end user, 'Go to hell.'"

It's practically a cliché to say that the key to persuasion is to put yourself in the buyer's shoes. And it's certainly sound advice. But the problem is, no one tells you *how* to understand what's in the buyer's mind. Michael Masterson's BDF formula gives you a three-step process for getting into the mind of your attendee. Before writing a persuasive speech or sales presentation, write out in narrative form the BDF of your target market. Share this with your meeting planner and get her input. Then write your talk based on the agreed BDF.

The Ultimate Secret to Successful Topic Selection

Another aspect of planning is choosing the topic of your presentation. In some cases, your speaking topic is determined for you; the boss wants a presentation updating her on the quarterly sales figures, or you are invited to speak on outsourcing at an industry conference. Then your challenge is to come up with a great slant, focus, hook, and title (see section below) for the presentation.

On the other hand, if you speak to publicize your business or product, promote public seminars, or make money as a part-time or full-time professional trainer, or just enjoy speaking to local groups as a hobby, you have to decide the topics you are going to present. How do you make that decision? Where do you start? By taking a personal inventory of your education, expertise, experience, knowledge, aptitudes, and interests:

- *Your education:* Not just your college major, but any special skills, trades, technology, processes, or other specialized subjects you've learned.

- *Your expertise:* What you know that others will pay money to learn from you.

- *Your experience:* What you have done that others want to learn how to do.

- *Your knowledge:* Wisdom and insights you've picked up in your decades of working and living that would benefit others.

- *Your aptitudes:* What you are good at and like to do.

- *Your interests:* What stimulates you, turns you on, engages your mind, body, and spirit; in other words, your passions.

Your speaking topic is determined in part by your desire—what you want to speak about—and in part by who you are—what you are qualified to speak about. When you are younger, you have more flexibility in choosing the knowledge you wish to acquire that can be the basis of your public speaking activities, your career, or any business you start. Older speakers have both an advantage and a disadvantage over their younger counterparts. Our advantage is that, having lived longer, we have accumulated more of everything: wisdom, knowledge, experience, stories, even jokes. And we can draw from this rich storehouse to add depth and verisimilitude to our talks.

But the older speaker also has a few disadvantages over younger presenters. One is that we are somewhat locked into our field of expertise. Having spent the last two or three decades honing our skills as a lawyer or a programmer or whatever, we are loath to abandon that investment to jump into a new subject that may be hotter and more in demand. Also, the younger generation is growing up with the newest technology from birth, while we are forced to learn it at an age where our brains are less flexible. Therefore, although we can learn and understand new technologies, they will never be as integrated into our lives and knowledge base as well as if we'd been using them all our lives, as younger people have.

For example, I have been a freelance copywriter specializing in direct marketing since 1982, so I am qualified to give talks on both copywriting and direct marketing. But today, those are not the hot topics in marketing. The hot topics in marketing are new developments such as search engine optimization (SEO), social networking, blogging, Web 2.0, and viral marketing. Now, I have studied, used, and understand many of these methods. But it is the younger generation of marketers, for the most part, who have embraced them wholeheartedly. I can and have learned many of these marketing methods, but I am not the best-qualified person to teach them.

Speaking on topics with which you have had significant experience enables you to draw on a rich source of stories that will be relevant and meaningful to your audience.

There are some topics that can be adequately taught by a trained speaker who is not an expert in the topic but studies up on it. Many other topics clearly beg to be taught by someone who is an experienced practitioner in the field. In this book, I assume you have or will acquire expertise; my goal is to make you an expert who is also a good speaker and teacher.

Many years ago, I attended an evening course at a local adult education program on mail order; I had a small mail order business and wanted ideas for improvement. Within one minute of the instructor opening her mouth, I and everyone in the class saw that she knew absolutely nothing about mail order, had no experience in mail order, and was simply reading out of an instructor's guide. It was embarrassing for her and a waste of the students' time and money.

While topics for lectures are theoretically limitless, they are somewhat limited to subjects that people will pay to learn. It's quite possible to get a lot of speaking invitations to talk about leadership, management, website design, e-commerce, or cost-based accounting. The audiences for obscure topics like the history of masking tape or collecting 15th-century Peruvian pottery are much smaller, and the opportunities to speak before groups interested in these subjects are few and far between.

Aristotle said words to the effect that your topic or area of specialization is defined by the intersection of your passions and the needs of the marketplace. Your quest for topic selection begins with what interests you. Make a list of your education, expertise, experience, knowledge, aptitudes, and interests. Examine the list. Put a check mark next to the items that the marketplace needs to know more about and will pay to learn. From that short list, pick one or two subjects; these form the basis of your first talks.

I said earlier that people will pay to hear talks on leadership, sales, motivation, management, small business, and other topics. But actually, these are becoming harder to sell today, because so many speakers are competing for the opportunity to give these programs. The solution is to narrow the focus and talk about a specialized area or segment of a broader topic, one that you know well.

A narrow topic is often better than a broad topic for several reasons. When you pick a broad topic like "safety," it's difficult to cover the subject

Advantages of Choosing a Narrow Topic

The more general a speaking topic is, the more speakers there are out there competing for the opportunity to present it. Conversely, if you speak on a highly technical topic, you can write your own ticket when it comes to offering yourself as a speaker, because so few people are qualified to teach it. You also have less competition when you focus on a narrow niche rather than speak on a broad topic.

adequately in a 20-minute lunch talk or even in a full-day course. So you need to narrow it down. You can narrow the topic either by focusing on one specific area or tailoring it for a specific audience or industry. For instance, a trainer hired to do a class on safety for a construction company could offer a program on "Meeting OSHA Requirements in the Construction Industry." An engineer speaking on his specialty, industrial gases, at a lunch meeting of the America Institute of Chemical Engineers might narrow the focus to "Safe Handling of Compressed Gas Cylinders."

Speaker Fred Gleeck advises speakers to choose niches rather than broad topics. Fred specializes in marketing—helping businesses get more customers—and has programs on marketing tailored to a dozen different niche markets; for instance, one of his programs is "Marketing for the Self-Storage Industry." Speaker Wally Bock defines a niche as the intersection of a topic (e.g., customer service) with an industry (e.g., banking). One of Fred's niches is marketing for the self-storage industry. He could have chosen marketing for dentists, but there are tons of speakers offering programs in that niche; in fact, there is a speaker's bureau that does nothing but handle dental speakers. But Fred has almost no competition in marketing for the self-storage industry; few speakers know it, and even fewer have any interest in learning it. The lack of competition allows Fred to command a premium price for training materials and programs in this niche market.

Writing a Compelling Title and Description for Your Talk

Presentations for workplace meetings often don't have a formal title, though it's not a bad idea to have one. If you are going to talk about plans to launch a new product, the title slide of your PowerPoint might be "Launch Plans for WebOptimizer Version 1.0." Having a specific title keeps participants on track and enables the speaker to cut off attendees who wander off on tangents by reminding them their rant is not related to the matter at hand.

Public seminars and private workshops need strong titles to attract meeting planners, training directors, and attendees. The title need not be flashy, though; sometimes, a straightforward title works best. For instance, my most popular training class is called simply "Effective Technical Writing." Brilliant? Hardly. Clear and effective? Definitely.

A good example of a simple but strong title is the first seminar given decades ago by my friend, fellow speaker Fred Gleeck. His first public seminar was on the topic of how to succeed as an independent consultant. The title, "Become a Successful Consultant in Your Own Field," is strong. It begins with an action verb (become), offers an implied benefit (you will learn to be successful), and is tailored to each attendee's individual background and interests (in your own field). Action words that imply a benefit work especially well in seminar titles. These include: reduce, lower, save, improve, enhance, manage, increase, boost, extend, maximize, minimize. The title slide of your presentation should contain the title of your presentation, the name of the speaker, his title and organization, and his website URL.

Using a number in the talk's title is also effective. I get large crowds whenever I give my presentation "17 Ways to Increase E-Mail Marketing Response Rates" at marketing conferences. One reason is that the title states a clear benefit the attendee desired: increasing e-mail marketing response rates. The second is the use of a number in the title. When a reader sees "17 ways to do X," she immediately makes a mental list of all the ways she can think of to do X. If it does not equal your number (e.g., she only comes up with 11 ways instead of 17), she wants to hear your talk to find out the additional ways. Even if her number matches yours, she wants to see whether her list is the same as yours—or whether it contains new ideas she doesn't know or hasn't tried.

Another approach to titles—one I am not personally a practitioner of, but others have had great success with—is to coin a term. Years ago, the consultant Mike Hammer wrote a book about "re-engineering" and by doing so invented a topic only he could speak on (or at least in which he was the pre-eminent speaker). Is inventing a term for your speech a good idea? If the term catches on, you, like Hammer, become the de facto guru on the topic, making it much easier to get speaking engagements. On the other hand, if the term doesn't catch fire with the public, it will generate little or no interest in having you speak on it.

The SAP Formula for Public Speaking

SAP (*subject, audience,* and *purpose*) is a quick and handy formula that speakers, writers, and other content providers can use when preparing to deliver information in any form.

- *Subject*: the topic on which you speak. Define it as clearly, specifically, and narrowly as possible (e.g., "safe handling of compressed gas cylinders" instead of "plant safety").

- *Audience*: who you will be speaking to, including the demographics, education, background, and interest (or lack of interest) in your topic as discussed earlier in this chapter.

- *Purpose*: the objective of the presentation—what you or the meeting planner want to happen as a result of the attendees hearing your talk.

The P of SAP, "purpose," surprises some presenters when I bring it up. Amazingly, they never think about their talking having a purpose. "I was asked to summarize the improvements done to the machine #3 in our custom extrusion operation," one engineer told me. "There is no 'purpose.' I just have to present the information."

But people in his company are busy. If there is no purpose to getting the information, why bother to have a meeting about it? Or why not just put it in a memo or post in on the company intranet? Clearly, there is some reason management wants the engineer and his audience to assemble in a room while they hear his report in person. Without defining the purpose through a SAP analysis, the objective is unlikely to be accomplished—and both the time spent preparing and delivering the talk, and the time spent listening to the talk, will have been wasted.

In question #8 in my Pre-Program Questionnaire, reprinted in Appendix II, I ask meeting planners to tell me their objectives for my talk, something you should do whenever you speak as well. What are the specific objectives for your speech? What skills should the attendees gain, what changes in attitude should take place, what actions do you want the audience to take as a result of attending your session?

This is not a trivial or theoretical consideration for the speaker; it is the crux of the entire speech. Thanks to the internet, information on just about any topic is easily obtained with a Google search. The reasons to have experts give lectures and speeches and training programs are to accomplish change and improvement; to help the attendees do their jobs better, live happier lives, increase their productivity, improve quality, or give better customer service. As we will explore in this book, a live training session by an expert speaker or facilitator can accomplish these objectives in ways printed, online, or broadcast content often cannot.

A Slice of a Slice

Just how narrow or broad should the topic for a talk be? Let's use the analogy of a pizza, which you can buy whole or in slices; some people, like my oldest son, like their slice cut in half—think of it as a slice of a slice. When you are writing a book on a topic, you can either give the reader the whole pizza or a slice. Let's say the topic is marketing. That's a broad topic, so I think of it as a whole pizza. Go to the bookstore, and you can find books that cover all aspects of marketing. With the glut of marketing books out there today, you might have a better chance of selling your book if you just tackled a slice of the topic of marketing; e.g., how to design an effective website.

But in a talk, the whole pizza or even the slice are often too much for your audience to digest in the limited time allotted. So rather than give a talk on "marketing" or "designing effective websites," you might focus in on a slice of the slice; a subset of the techniques used in creating an effective website; e.g., "keyword research and discovery" or "writing web page meta tags that increase search engine rankings."

When your speaking topic is too broad, you set yourself a difficult challenge and risk giving a talk crammed with too much information for you to deliver or your audience to absorb. With a narrower, better-defined, more specific topic—a slice of a slice—you can comfortably cover the subject adequately in the time allotted, giving your listeners solid value, practical tips, and actionable ideas.

I discuss elsewhere in this book the notion that you don't have to deliver a huge number of ideas or tips to make your talk worthwhile for your audience. And it's true: If I gain even one new idea from a talk I hear, it almost always pays back my investment in time and money to attend the workshop many times over. Well, here's a little technique for making sure your listeners understand this notion and agree that you have delivered on it.

"Limit your remarks to three main points. People remember things that come in threes."

- Alan Sharpe

Early in my talk, right after the introduction and before I get into the meat of the material, I tell the audience that my goal is to give them at least one new idea or technique they can use. I then ask them if they would consider the presentation worthwhile if I can do that, and of course, they all agree.

During my lectures, I usually give a dozen or so tips or ideas, and of course, usually one or two are my favorites; the ones I think are most valuable and that the listener is unlikely to have heard before. When I get to the best tip, I give it, and then say to the audience: "If you only do one thing we've covered here today, this is the one you should do." When I get to the second best tip, I say, "If you do TWO things we've covered here today, in addition to tip #1, this should be the second." In my close, I remind them of what those two tips are.

The value in this technique is twofold: First, it helps prompt the audience members to take action, put what they have learned to work, and actually do something, which is the only way my presentation can have real value for them. Second, I have already gotten their agreement that if they only get one great actionable tip from my talk, they got their money's worth; this technique demonstrates to them that they have gotten at least two such tips—more than their money's worth.

I think it's important for you to use this technique or otherwise motivate your audience not just to listen to your lecture or take notes on it, but also to actually do something with the information. You know that if you don't read

Take Notes:

Be aware that the meeting planner's and audience's interests may not be identical. The attendees might be IT professionals hoping to learn a new technology so their skills stay current and they remain marketable during a job search; the director of IT training is more interested in helping the company increase productivity and efficiency through adaptation of a new computer system, platform, or application.

the Sunday newspaper by Tuesday, you never get to it and end up throwing the whole thing in the trash. Workshops and seminars are similar. If a group hears you speak on Saturday, they will forget 90 percent of what you told them within a week. Further, if they don't start using at least one of the techniques you taught by Monday or Tuesday, they never will.

Researching the Venue and Event

The most important preparation steps to take before you give a talk are SAP: To thoroughly understand the *subject* you are there to present; the *audience* and their needs, interests, and concerns; and the *purpose*, both of the meeting planner hiring you to talk and the audience attending your talk.

Other pre-presentation research includes finding out details of the event at which you are speaking. Is it a sales conference? Distributors rally for a multi-level marketing (MLM) company? Breakout workshop for an internet marketing conference? Who is coming, and what are their expectations? Ask the meeting planner why people are coming and what they hope to get out of the event in general and your talk in particular.

You also should research the *venue,* or location. Are you speaking in a conference room at the company headquarters? Or in the ballroom of a resort hotel on the beach in Florida? Sometimes you will be surprised, and not always pleasantly. Once, I was invited to give a technical writing class for engineers at a chemical company. When I got to the plant early in the morning, no one was there but the security guard, who led me to a dingy classroom in the basement. There was little heat and poor lighting; it was dark, depressing, shabby, and not terribly clean, and there was no easel, flip chart, or markers as I had requested. I had to scramble to collect everything and ready the room so that when attendees shuffled in at 8 A.M. yawning and drinking their morning coffee, I was cheerful, composed, and ready to teach.

Also, ask the meeting planner how the audience members are likely to be dressed. Most companies have dress codes, either business attire or business casual, and most conferences specify appropriate attire in their pre-conference attendee's kit. My rule of thumb is to dress one level above the audience. If the audience is dressed business casual, I wear a suit and tie. For a conference held at a tropical beach resort where the attendees are wearing shorts, Hawaiian shirts, and sandals, I might wear business casual. But I will wear a nice blazer, and have a tie in the pocket just in case people come in better dressed than was anticipated.

Assessing your Communications Environment

Whenever and wherever you speak, even if it's your own company, arrive at the location and check out the room where you'll be speaking at least 30 minutes and preferably 60 minutes before you are scheduled to take the stage or go to the platform.

All speakers, including me, can tell you absolute nightmare stories about speaking venues. A classic scenario: A speaker whose talk is focused around a series of short videos requests a DVD player and monitor early, and reminds the meeting planner about this several times. Of course, when he gets to the room, no DVD player or monitor is in sight.

The size of the room, seating arrangements, and acoustics are important. For corporate training, I prefer to have attendees sitting in chairs at tables, facing the front of the room. I am at the front, where there is a podium to stand behind and rest my notes on, and a table next to it where I can place my handouts. The room is also equipped with an LCD projector and screen to show the PowerPoint from my laptop. Although I use a podium, I don't stay behind it for long; I prefer to walk out into the room and pass close by my students.

Lighting and temperature are also important. In a long session, especially after a meal, a too-dim room can cause audience members to get sleepy, lose attention, or even nod off. Keep the lights as bright as you can without making the PowerPoint on the screen difficult to read. As for temperature, there is never agreement among attendees; one complains of being too warm, while another says she is freezing. As a rule, it's better to err on the side of keeping the room too cool rather than too warm. Cool air keeps people awake, but warmth, like dark, can make them sleepy.

Unless you are promoting your own public seminars, you often have little or no control over food and beverages. If you are promoting your own public seminars, food and beverage expenses can quickly get out of control and eat up your profits. For a morning talk, there should always be coffee; and doughnuts, pastries, fruit, or some other breakfast foods are also a good idea. In a full-day class or workshop, you can let the group seek lunch on their own, provided the hotel has a restaurant or there is one nearby, and these restaurants can quickly accommodate a group your size. Coffee should be available throughout the day, as should water; and put out soft drinks in the afternoon.

Some meeting planners tailor the menu to the group, only to find their efforts come to naught. For instance, I gave a weekend seminar to a group of marketing managers at a company that promoted nutritional supplements and health foods. For Sunday morning breakfast, the meeting planner had healthy foods like yogurt, granola, and fruit on one side of the buffet table; on the other was the usual bacon, eggs, pancakes, and sausage. I paid careful attention to everyone's choice. Later, when making a point about believing in

Prevent Calendar Conflicts That Keep Your Audience Away

Check the calendar carefully to make sure no major holiday or event conflicts with the scheduled date of your talk. Interfering events include religious holidays, school events (proms, graduations, vacations), sporting events (the World Series, the Super Bowl), and business or industry activities (e.g., a major trial for a law firm or tax preparation season for an accounting firm).

what you are selling, I told them I had surveyed their choices at breakfast, and asked them to guess what percentage had taken only the healthy breakfast vs. the unhealthy breakfast alone vs. a combination of both. They were shocked at the answer: 100 percent had partaken of the bacon and eggs, either by itself or in combination with healthier choices.

Often the room is too small or the sponsor has more attendees than they expected, so modifications have to be made in a hurry, chairs brought in, tables moved. When the room is too large, attendees tend to avoid the front rows, perhaps for fear of being called on, and sit toward the back and in the

Take Notes:

You should always attribute material you adapt or research from other sources, and strive to make your content as original as possible. However, there are many times during a talk that you have to think on your feet, ad lib, or come up with a response or answer on the fly. Occasionally in these situations, we speakers may inadvertently plagiarize material from a source. My solution is to acknowledge the source after I have blurted the comment; e.g., "I didn't write that joke, by the way. I think I either saw it in a cartoon in *The New Yorker* or heard it on David Letterman." Acknowledge sources as accurately and as often as you can.

I've heard some speakers give talks that are little more than bits and pieces of books, articles, and lectures strung together. Avoid being this kind of copycat speaker. If everything you say is taken from another speaker or author, you can just hand out a bibliography and leave; the audience can get it from the original source and has no need to see and hear you. Naturally, you can strengthen your talks and writings by quoting other sources or incorporating other people's words and ideas when appropriate. But these should be used to illuminate, illustrate, and reinforce your own ideas and recommendations. No one needs to hear you give a rehash of Tom Peters or Anthony Robbins, a mistake amateur and new speakers frequently make.

middle. Before I start, I ask them several times to move up so they can hear and see better.

You can rarely do much about the acoustics or sound system, but be aware of it, just the same. If there are sound problems, ask the audience whether they can hear you, and make an extra effort to speak clearly and not too rapidly. Also, go with the flow. Once, my lecture was interrupted several times by the sound from a talk in an adjoining room spilling over into my room's sound system. The other talk was on surgery, and was quite graphic. I made a small joke in reference to it, and from then on, whenever the surgery talk piped up on our sound system again, it became a source of amusement rather than frustration or annoyance.

I had to think fast and wasn't prepared for being interrupted by a loud lecture on gall bladder operations, so I told a short joke that popped into my memory; the source was either a *New Yorker* cartoon or David Letterman's top ten list. The joke: "What's the one thing you never want to hear in the operating room when you're about to be put under for surgery?" Answer: "Please accept this sacrifice, oh Lord of Darkness."

Test the sound system and the room acoustics before you speak. When you start, ask the people in the back of the room whether they can hear you okay, even if you are using a microphone. Also, put up your flip charts or PowerPoint slides, step to the back of the room, and make sure they are readable. If not, ask people to move up, or if that fails, be sure to explain and read what is on the slide, and offer to send an electronic or hard copy after the presentation to anyone who requests it.

Getting Up To Speed on Audience Hot Buttons

In every industry and field, there are "hot buttons." These are major issues of concern to the majority of people in the business. Some hot buttons, such as complying with EPA regulations, are ongoing concerns. Others, like the sub-prime mortgage crisis, are temporary conditions. Either way, speakers must be aware of the hot buttons. Even if your talk doesn't deal with them directly, you need to know what's foremost in the audience's minds when you speak. And you should inject a reference or two to one or more of the hot buttons in every talk.

How do you learn the audience's hot buttons? You can start with a Google search and read a few recent issues of the leading trade journal covering that field. Reading a newspaper can also bring you up to date on news and events important to your audience. My Pre-Program Questionnaire (see Appendix II) can also help here. Question 5 on the form asks the meeting planner to define the three most pressing challenges or problems faced by members of the group; question 7 asks what the three most significant events or trends have been during the last year in their industry or within their company or group. Between them, the answers to these two questions will reveal the audience's key hot buttons.

Gain Confidence and Add Great Content to Your Talk

Years ago, I was asked to give a speech on marketing at a convention of dentists. It was the only time in my career I was speaking to a market I really didn't know well and failed to research the market sufficiently. I thought I knew what dentists wanted. But when I got to the convention, I realized that I was the only speaker there who was not a dentist. For the first time in a long time, I felt unprepared and anxious.

Unknowingly, the meeting planner saved me. He said a number of the dentists were hoping to get some free consulting from me, and would I mind spending about 20 minutes each with a half a dozen or so of the attendees? During those six private sessions, I asked the dentists what marketing problems they had, what marketing programs they have tried, and which had worked and which had flopped—and I took a lot of notes when they spoke. During the lunch break before my speech, I sequestered myself in an empty conference room and rapidly updated and revised my talk. I added marketing stories I'd heard from the dentists I'd interviewed. During my talk, I told these stories. Since they all seemed to know one another, I referenced the source, saying things like, "This morning, I talked with Pam from Dr. Brown's office, and here's an interesting mailing approach that worked for them."

The audience loved it. They were impressed by the seemingly in-depth research I had done (which they assume I had conducted months in advance), and the interviews with their peers. Because of those interviews, I felt more confident in my ability to relate to the audience. The lesson I learned was that to deliver a speech to a niche market does not require total immersion in that market; if you are a quick study, a few interviews with people in the target market or group can be more than sufficient.

From that point on, I routinely began to ask meeting planners and training directors, both for my association presentations and corporate training programs, to give me the names of a few audience members I can speak with to get a feel for who they are and what they want to know. One of the attendees I interview should be someone who is popular, respected, and well known to the group. During the interview, I invariably pick up a good idea or two to add to my talk. When I get to the idea, I say, "This is something Dan told me in a phone call a month or so ago." This has two benefits. First, Dan is flattered that I referenced him aloud and becomes a more active participant in the session. Second, the other attendees listen more closely because, although they don't know me, they know and respect Dan.

Later in the book, we'll talk specifically about butterflies (speaking anxiety) and how to deal with that problem. But interviewing a few attendees in advance is one of the best techniques I know for getting over your fear of speaking. By borrowing a solid idea or two from a known member of the group, you also borrow his credibility. Your audience thinks, "The speaker is quoting Jerry; Jerry really knows his stuff; so the speaker must also really know his stuff." Another advantage is that, should you be challenged on this point, Jerry is likely to jump in and defend his own idea, taking the heat off you.

Knowing Your Audience = Speaking Success

CHAPTER 3

Organizing Your Talk

> Experts don't necessarily know more than everybody else - but their information is better organized.

Even if you are a great speaker, your audience will be uncomfortable and dissatisfied unless you present your material in a well-organized, logical fashion. As Jerry Bachetti, a technical editor, notes: "If your information is well organized, the audience can understand it even if your presentation is not that clear. But if the information is poorly organized, forget it; there's no way for them to make sense of it."

For me, the most important task of speaking is preparation of the outline. The outline tells me what points I have to cover, in how much depth, and in what order. Also, meeting planners frequently want an outline of your topic to put in their printed agenda, promotional mailings, and conference workbooks. When asked by meeting planners for an outline of the key points to be covered, many speakers hastily jot a few quick bullets of the first things that pop into their mind, shoot them off to the meeting planner in a quick e-mail, and then promptly forget about them.

Weeks later, when they sit down to prepare their presentation, these speakers realize they have painted themselves into a corner because the outline doesn't work. Often, by then, the conference invitations have already been mailed and it's too late to change them. They are then faced with the unpleasant task of having to deliver a talk in an order that makes little sense and does not communicate their topic in a logical fashion.

You may be thinking: Why can't the speaker just write the talk he wants to deliver, and then explain to the audience prior to starting that he has made some changes? The reason is that when people attend a presentation, their expectation is that the speaker will cover every item listed in the seminar description in the order listed. Trust me on this. I have promoted public seminars during which attendees have told me they came primarily to learn just one of the bullet items listed in the program. You cannot just jot a bulleted agenda casually.

Every subtopic you promise in the seminar description, you must cover in your presentation.

For these reasons, I am extremely careful about creating a sensible, detailed outline for my talk before I begin to put the presentation together. I am equally careful about writing the seminar description. A seminar description is a short overview of the program you intend to present. I create and store seminar descriptions for all my talks as Word files in a subdirectory on my PC. When I am asked to speak, I can cut and paste the seminar description into an e-mail and submit it to the meeting planner in seconds.

A standard seminar description has four basic parts: The title, a description or overview, an agenda (a bullet list of major topics covered), and a brief speaker bio. Some meeting planners may ask you to provide additional information in your seminar description; e.g., a list of common questions about the topic you will answer in your session, or a list of the knowledge or skills you guarantee the attendee will acquire after listening to your talk. A sample seminar description is reprinted in Appendix III.

Content vs. Salesmanship

In business, a vast majority of presentations have some sort of persuasive element. Sales presentations and product demonstrations are blatantly promotional. But even informational talks have a persuasive component: You are often selling the audience on accepting an idea, method, or technology you want them to follow or use; or attempting to change a belief, opinion, or attitude they hold.

Of course, your objective is to sell. But be careful. People attending a luncheon or dinner meeting aren't there to be sold. They want to be entertained. Informed. Educated. Made to laugh or smile. Selling your product, service, or company may be your goal, but in public speaking, it has to be secondary to giving a good presentation, and a "soft-sell" approach works best.

The amount of selling you can do depends on the venue. An unfortunate trend in conferences, workshops, seminars, and "boot camps" is that some speakers, instead of delivering useful content, spend most of their presentation time bragging about their success and then selling attendees an expensive package of their training materials. Many attendees quite rightly complain that they paid the rather stiff registration fee to learn, not to hear a sales pitch. If you speak at a boot camp or conference for an hour, you should deliver a 50-minute presentation with five to ten minutes for questions and answers. Your sales pitch, if any, should be limited to no more than one minute after the talk and before the Q&A.

Of course, many presentations are primarily informative, not persuasive. Terry C. Smith, author of *Making Successful Presentations* (John Wiley & Sons), lists the following as possible objectives for business presentations:

- inform or instruct

- persuade or sell

- make recommendations and gain acceptance

- arouse interest

- inspire or initiate action

- evaluate, interpret, and clarify

- set the stage for further action

- gather ideas and explore them

- entertain.

I'd add "establish credibility" to this list; a good talk can go a long way toward building the image of the speaker and his or her firm as authorities in the field. "Perhaps you are aiming for a combination of these," says Smith. "For example, there is nothing wrong with being both informative and entertaining; the two are not mutually exclusive. In fact, the two may complement one another."

Let's say your talk is primarily informational. You could organize it along the following lines: First, an introduction that presents an overview of the topic; next, the body of the talk, which presents the facts in detail; finally, a conclusion that sums up for the audience what they have heard. This repetition is beneficial because, in a spoken presentation, unlike an article, listeners cannot flip back to a preceding page or paragraph to refresh their memory or study your material in more detail. For this reason, you must repeat your main point at least three times to make sure it is understood and remembered.

And what if your talk is primarily persuasive or sales oriented? In their book *How to Make Speeches for All Occasions* (Doubleday), Harold and Marjorie Zelko present the following outline for a persuasive talk:

1. Draw attention to the subject.

2. Indicate the problem, need, or situation.

3. Analyze the problem's origin, history, causes, and manifestations.

4. Lead toward possible solutions, or mention them.

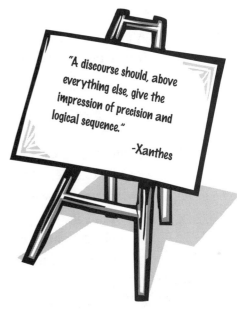

5. Lead toward most desired solution or action.

6. Offer proof and values of solution proposed.

7. Prove it as better than other solutions. Prove it will eliminate causes of problems, will work, and has value.

8. Lead toward desired response from audience.

9. Show how desired response can be realized.

10. Conclude by summary and appeal as appropriate.

Janet Stone and Jane Bachner present a similar outline for persuasive organization in their book, *Speaking Up* (McGraw-Hill):

1. Secure attention of audience.

2. State the problem.

3. Prove the existence of the problem.

4. Describe the unfortunate consequences of the problem.

5. State your solution.

6. Show how your solution will benefit the audience.

7. Anticipate and answer objections you know are coming.

8. Invite action.

A popular organizational scheme for any type of persuasive presentation, from a political speech to ad copy is the five-step "motivating sequence."

Step 1: Get attention. Before you can begin to communicate, you have to get the audience's attention. Your opening must get the listener to stop fidgeting, sit up straight, focus on your visuals, and listen to what you are saying. You already know many methods of getting attention, and see dozens of examples of them in action every day, such as in TV and magazine advertising where sex is often used to gain attention for products ranging from soft drinks and cars to diets and exercise programs. You can make a bold statement, cite a startling statistic, ask a curiosity-arousing question, make a loud noise, or use a bold graphic or a prop. You get the idea.

Step 2: Identify the problem or need. Most products fill a need or solve a problem that a group of prospects are facing. But what are the chances that the prospect is thinking about this problem at this second? Not great. So in selling situations, you have to focus the prospect's attention on the need or problem your product addresses. Only then can you talk to them about a solution. For instance, if you are giving a sales presentation selling an economical office telephone system, instead of starting off by talking about your system, you might ask your audience members, "Are your telephone bills too high?"

Step 3: Position your product, service, or organization as the solution to the problem. Once you get the prospect to focus on the problem, the next step is to position your product or service as the solution to that problem. This can be a quick transition; here's an example from a fundraising letter from the Red Cross:

> *Dear Mr. Bly:*
> *Some day, you may need the Red Cross.*
> *But right now, the Red Cross needs you.*

Step 4: Proof. As Mark Joyner points out in his book *The Irresistible Offer* (John Wiley & Sons, 2005), one of the questions at the tip of your prospect's tongue upon receiving your promotion is, "Why should I believe you?" You answer that question by offering proof. That proof is of two sorts.

The first type of proof goes to credibility. It convinces the prospect that you, the seller, are a reputable firm or individual, and therefore someone to be trusted. A diploma from a prestigious medical school displayed prominently on a doctor's office wall is an example of proof of credibility.

The second type of proof has to do with the product, and convinces the buyer that your product can do what you say it can do. Testimonials, case histories, reviews, performance graphs, and test results are examples of proof in this category. A demonstration, either live or on video, can also be convincing.

Step 5: Action. The final step is to ask for action. Your goal is usually to generate either an inquiry or an order. To ask for action in sales presentations, we make an "offer." For instance, if we are selling a software product we have just demonstrated during our presentation, the offer may be a 30-day free trial of the software.

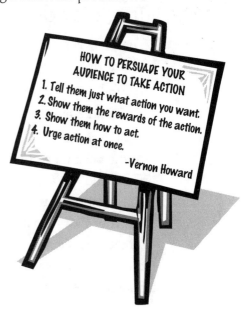

The motivational sequence, while ideal for persuasive presentations, is just one of many organizational schemes available to speakers. For instance, if you're describing a process, your talk can be organized along the natural flow of the process or the sequence of steps involved in completing it. This would be ideal for a talk entitled "How to Start Your Own Dog Sitting Service" or "How to Design Mixers for Viscous Fluids."

If you're talking about expanding a communications network worldwide, you might start with the United States, then move on to Asia, then cover Europe. If your topic is vitamins and minerals, covering them in alphabetical order from vitamin A to zinc seems a sensible approach.

I allow at least one full day for preparation and rehearsal of any new short (20- to 30-minute) talk. Terry Smith says that for every brand-new presentation, his ratio is one hour of preparation for every minute he plans to speak. "This is the preparation level at which I feel comfortable that I'm giving my very best," says Smith.

The trick to reducing preparation time is to have two or three "canned" (standard) talks that you can offer to various audiences. Even with a canned presentation, you'll need at least several hours to analyze the audience, do some customizing of your talk to better address that particular group, and rehearse once or twice. Once you have PowerPoint presentations for three or more standard presentations, you can quickly and easily customize new talks largely by combining and rearranging existing slides from these PowerPoint presentations, and then adding any new slides required.

The 3 Ts Speaking Formula

The "3 Ts Formula" for organizing any speech is old advice but good advice. This formula says that in every talk, you should:

1. Tell your attendees what you are going to tell them.
2. Tell them.
3. Tell them what you told them.

At the beginning of your talk, you outline the points you are going to cover. The middle is a presentation of these points. Toward the close, just before you finish, sum up the points they just learned.

Your slides can mirror this organizational scheme. In my PowerPoint presentations, the first slide (after the title slide) is a bulleted or numbered list of the major points I plan to cover, in the order in which I will cover them. The middle slides help illustrate and present the major points. After that, and right before the close, I insert the first slide again—the slide I used at the beginning to preview the talk—as my wrap-up for the talk. By using the identical slide to tell them what I am going to tell them in the beginning (step one of the 3 Ts Formula) and tell them what I told them at the end (step three), they can clearly see that I covered everything I said I would. This helps all attendees, but especially the nitpickers and anal retentives, see that they clearly got what I promised.

Choosing your Organizational Scheme

The 3 Ts Formula gives you a broad outline that can cover many different types of presentations. However, you still have to decide how to organize the material in step two of the formula: What you actually are telling them. Often, the organizational scheme is a matter of choice, and you can organize your talk in whatever sequence suits your fancy. Other times, the nature of your content suggests an organizational scheme that is clearly better than other options:

- *Order of location.* A science lecture on the planets of the solar system might begin with Mercury (the planet nearest the sun) and end with Pluto (the dwarf planet farthest out). A presentation on a new nationwide network of storage depots could likewise be in order of location.

- *Order of increasing difficulty.* When teaching a skill or process, it's often best to start with the easiest material and, as the students master basic principles, move on to more complex operations. In a full-day training class, you can begin with an easy task or skill they can master by midmorning. This gives the attendees a sense of accomplishment, and they feel that even if they were to learn nothing more the rest of the day, the class was worth attending.

- *Alphabetical order.* A logical way to arrange a lecture on vitamins (A, B, B1, and so on), dietary supplements, zoo animals, countries, or any other subject with multiple topics that can be ordered in an A to Z fashion.

- *Chronological order.* Presents the facts in the order in which they happened. Lectures about travel, expeditions, historical, or current events are often organized this way. So are case histories, personal narratives, and success stories about how the speaker made good in the face of adversity.

- *Problem/solution.* Another format appropriate to case histories and many types of reports. The problem/solution format begins with "Here's what the problem was" and ends with "Here's how we solved it."

- *Inverted pyramid.* The newspaper style of news reporting where the lead paragraph summarizes the story and the following paragraphs present the facts in order of decreasing importance. You can use this format in some talks, most notably executive briefings.

- *Deductive order.* Start with a generalization, and then support it with particulars. Scientists use this format in research papers that begin with the findings and then state the supporting evidence. In a speech, you start by stating your hypothesis, belief, or principles, and then pile on facts that prove your assertion. My friend Robert Lerose used this approach in an award-winning essay he wrote on same-sex marriage. He stated at the outset that he believed in same-sex marriages, and then gave extensive proof in defense of his position. Trial lawyers use this method in the courtroom: You know right up front whether they are trying to prove the defendant innocent or guilty, and then all of their arguments and proof are brought to bear on proving their position.

- *Inductive order.* Begin with specific instances, and then lead the attendee to the ideas or general principles the instances suggest. This is an excellent way to keep high school and college students interested and engaged. You tell a series of fascinating facts and anecdotes, which lead inexorably to an inescapable conclusion. When you finally state the principles and ideas the examples illustrate, the listener has an "A-ha" moment and accepts them as truth, since he has just heard numerous examples that prove the point. This is an especially useful organizational scheme for giving a talk supporting a belief or position about which some members of the audience might be skeptical and difficult to convince; e.g., a talk on the causes of global warming or funding a multi-billion dollar NASA project to land a person on Mars.

■ *List.* As discussed earlier, you can list the main points or ideas you intend to cover in your presentation in one-two-three fashion, and then cover them in that order. List presentations are easy to write, straightforward to deliver, and well received by audiences. When the title of your session has a number in it (e.g., "Seven Ways to Reduce Your Property Tax Payments," or "Five Common Gardening Mistakes to Avoid), the listener immediately wants to hear what those seven ways or five mistakes are.

How to End a Speech

"How should you end your speech? End it with the same sense of drama, emotion, humor, excitement with which you began it. End with a joke, a memorable quotation, a rhetorical question, a call to action. It's your choice. But the point is to go out like a lion, leaving the audience in a state that is somewhere between shock and delight."

"Have you ever noticed how a good play will end? Bang! The lights go out. The curtain comes down. For a second, the audience is stunned. They knew it was going to end soon, but they didn't quite expect it at that moment. There's a pause. Then suddenly they realize that yes, that was the perfect place to end it. And their applause erupts like a thunderclap. That's the way a speech should end!"

—Richard Armstrong, speechwriter

Making the Organizational Scheme Visible to the Audience

Some speakers like to make the organizational scheme of their talk apparent to the audience. They believe it helps the audience follow along better. Others use one or more of the above organizational schemes, but do not explicitly state they are doing so. My approach: When I am organizing the material as a numbered list or in alphabetical order, I tell the audience this is what I am doing, making it easier for them to follow along. With the other organizational schemes, I don't say how I am organizing the material. With those organizational methods, telling the listener would cause them to focus on figuring out whether the speaker is following it, rather than the content. If your presentation is organized using inductive or deductive reasoning, do not reveal this to the audience. Many of them do not understand these terms, so you'd just confuse them. And making the logic of these presentations too transparent robs them of some of their impact.

Deciding What You Should Include—And What to Leave Out

A full day gives you sufficient time to talk about your topic in depth. But most talks are an hour in length or less. To a new speaker, especially one with stage fright, an hour on the platform may seem like an eternity. But in reality, it's not very much time at all.

Right now, you are reading a book on public speaking. It's not a big or thick book, but it is over 70,000 words. By comparison, your average speaker talks at a rate of about 120 words a minute. So a 20-minute luncheon talk is around 2,400 words; a one-hour keynote speech is about 7,200 words. That's approximately one tenth of the word count of this book. So you see that even in a one-hour talk titled "Become a Better Public Speaker," I can't possibly cover more than a fraction of what's in this book.

Therefore, the brevity of most speeches requires great selectivity. You must select a limited number of points to cover. Let's say you are giving a lunch talk to last 20 minutes, and your topic is "Ten Tips to Improve Your Time Management Skills." You only have two minutes per tip. Actually, you have less than that, since you need time for a brief introduction and a short wrap-up and ending. With less than two minutes per tip, you don't have time enough for great detail, technical analysis, background, history, or in-depth discussion. You have just enough time to explain the tip clearly, tell the audience how to apply it in their work or lives, and maybe give a quick example.

Does that mean your talk has to be a straight presentation of content? No, because you'd be at risk of boring your audience. Monotonous speakers are dull. If you are giving lots of content, you have to mix it up with humor, stories, and some audience interaction.

You can't go off into long tangents, because there isn't time, and doing so is a turn off to attendees who are busy and came for content. But you can take some side roads. Throw in a few stories; either ones you've heard, ones that actually happened to you, or ones that are made-up but help illustrate a concept. A lecture that is a straightforward recitation of facts, theories, or principles can come across as abstract. To make your subject come alive for your audience, give examples, illustrations, and brief case studies. Don't tell jokes if you are not good at it. On the other hand, if you have a good sense of humor, a joke can help keep your audience interested and amused. People who are laughing are usually more receptive to your ideas and advice.

Use an Odd Number of Speech Points

Experience shows using odd numbers in presentation titles attracts more attendees than even numbers. Why? It's not clear. One possible explanation is that an even number seems neat and complete, while an odd number is more credible. Whatever the reason, "Seven Ways" seems to work better than "Eight Ways" or "Six Ways." The exception is ten, which also works well, e.g., "Top Ten" lists. The minimum title number is three. If there are just two tips, don't use a number title. Same with one tip; instead use a title such as "The Biggest Mistake in Doing X and How to Avoid It."

Using Bonus Content

Often but not always, I clearly number the major points. Also often but not always, I use that number in the title of the presentation; e.g., "Ten Ways to Improve Your Technical Writing." If I promise ten tips, however, I put an

Calculating Optimum Content Delivered Per Minute (CDPM) for your talk

The average speaker talks at a rate of around 120 words a minute. If you type up your presentation script word for word (something I'm not in favor of, as you will see in Chapter 4), you can fit approximately 250 words per page. The specifications for common lengths of presentations are shown below.

Speech Length in Time and Words

Presentation length	Number of words	Number of double-spaced typed pages (approx)
20 minutes	2,400	10
30 minutes	3,600	15
45 minutes	5,400	22
60 minutes	7,200	29
90 minutes	10,800	43
Half-day (3 hours)	21,600	86
Full day (6 hours)	43,200	173

eleventh tip and sometimes even twelfth one in the presentation, labeling them as "bonus tips." "These are tips you didn't pay for," I tell the audience in a good-natured way, which always gets a chuckle or at least an appreciative smile. So they can clearly see that not only did they get their money's worth; they got more than their money's worth. That, by the way, is a key to creating satisfied customers in any business or profession, for any product or service: Don't give the buyers their money's worth; give them more than their money's worth. Putting a bonus tip in your presentation is an admittedly transparent but wholly effective way to give the audience more than they bargained for.

Pace and Timing

Timing—completing my talk at a sensible pace within the allotted time—has always been a problem for me. Inexperienced speakers also find timing difficult. That makes sense, when you think about it: Not being experienced speakers, and perhaps giving a particular presentation in front of a live audience for the first time, you really have no idea how long it will take to get through your material.

So during the talk you are mentally evaluating where you are in the progression of your talk, and how much more material you have against the time remaining on the clock, which causes anxiety and uneven pacing. You slow down because you fear finishing too soon and before you know it, you have fallen behind. So you rush through the rest of the material to get it all in.

Are pace and timing important? Extremely. When you rush, the audience senses your panic, and becomes uneasy. Also, you may condense your material, creating an oral presentation that is too dense and fast-paced, and less than clear. On the other hand, when you are too slow, the listener's mind races ahead, because you are not talking nearly as fast as she is thinking.

Equally important as pace is staying within the allotted time. I have seen many otherwise fine speakers ignore this rule, always to their detriment.

Most people in the audience are quite time conscious. They worry about getting to the next session on time, or to their next meeting, or getting back to the office to get their work done. When you are in the final minutes of your allotted time, and they sense you are not even close to being done and have no intention of finishing on time, they become uncomfortable; their attention shifts from your material to their watches.

At a conference or other venue where you are one of many speakers and there are more sessions following yours, going over your allotted time can put the entire event off schedule, creating a huge problem for both the meeting planner and the attendees. It is also grossly unfair to other speakers, who have invested a lot in preparation and getting to the venue, only to be prevented from delivering their material because you took their time. As an example, I was asked to give a one-hour presentation on a topic with another speaker in Washington, DC. We were supposed to split the time equally. But he took a full 50 minutes. To my amazement, the meeting planner, who had introduced us and was sitting in the room, said nothing. So I had driven eight hours (round trip) to speak for ten minutes. Fortunately, attendees gave high marks to my presentations, and when the group invited me back to speak at the next year's conference, I was given a full hour by myself.

That brings up the question: What happens if you can't finish in the time available to you? If the speaker before you goes over the time limit, as happened to me in DC, and the meeting planner is not present, make sure you finish your segment by the scheduled time, even if that cuts you short. As I mentioned, attendees are very time conscious, and are unhappy when speakers and sessions run over.

You might think it's a good idea to poll the audience and ask whether they want you to finish on time or keep going for another 10 or 15 minutes. But be warned: I've had this backfire, with the vote split down the middle; half the room wanted to end on time, the other half wanted me to go longer. So I assured myself of automatically ignoring the wishes of and displeasing half the room. If the meeting planner is in the room, make the decision her

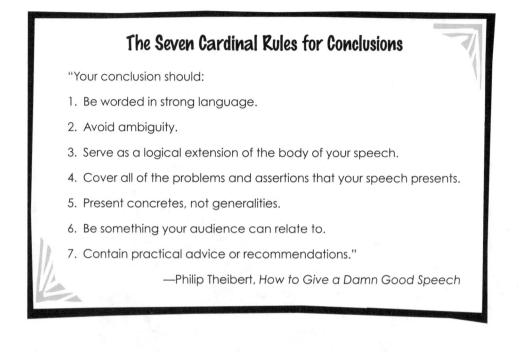

The Seven Cardinal Rules for Conclusions

"Your conclusion should:

1. Be worded in strong language.

2. Avoid ambiguity.

3. Serve as a logical extension of the body of your speech.

4. Cover all of the problems and assertions that your speech presents.

5. Present concretes, not generalities.

6. Be something your audience can relate to.

7. Contain practical advice or recommendations."

—Philip Theibert, *How to Give a Damn Good Speech*

responsibility. From the platform, say, "I see Dana there. Dana, do you want me to finish at noon, or go until 12:15¢"

For speakers who have difficulty determining how much material they can get through in a given amount of time, here's a technique that has worked for me. As you prepare your presentation prior to the date of the speech, find a point in your PowerPoint slides about two-thirds through the presentation where you are transitioning to a new point. Add a box to the top of that slide with text that says: "Optional Material if Time Allows; Otherwise, Read at Home." When you get to that slide, look at the time remaining. If you are nearly out of time, say, "And here's some additional material which you can keep as a reference or read at home." Make sure everyone has a copy of your slides, and if not, offer to send it electronically to anyone who asks. On the other hand, if you get to the "Optional Material" slide and there is enough time to get through the remaining slides, just keep going.

"Obviously the work of a cereal killer!"

At times, finding the right organizational scheme
for your content can be a real killer!

CHAPTER 4

Writing Your Presentation

THREE APPROACHES
TO SPEECH PREPARATION:
1. Write out the speech word for word.
2. Write speaker notes.
3. Speak "off the cuff."

ow do you create a presentation that wows your audience while achieving your objectives? There are three basic approaches to speech preparation:

1.   Writing out the speech word for word.

2.   Writing speaker notes.

3.   Speaking "off the cuff."

The first two are obvious. The third, speaking "off the cuff," means the speaker has the ability to step up to the platform with little or no preparation, and talk on given topic off the top of his head. Most speakers who can speak off the cuff are able to do so because of repetition and practice. They have talked on a particular subject so many times that, without deliberately making an effort to do so, they have practically memorized their basic speech. Subject matter experts who know their topic extremely well and are polished speakers with good memories may also be able to deliver off-the-cuff talks.

Word for Word or Speaker Notes

You can choose whichever of the above options works best for you. But in my opinion, Option 2—writing out and speaking from notes—works best for most speakers for a couple reasons. First, a good set of speaker notes keeps you on track, showing you what you have to cover, in the order you must cover it. Second, you can make your notes as detailed or as cursory as you want. My speaker notes are often a simple outline, to which I add specific notes about stories, facts, and lessons I want to be sure to include.

Unlike a written speech, in which an anecdote would be written out word for word, my speaker's notes might say no more than "Boots Story" to remind me to tell a story relating to customer service when I ordered a pair of boots from a mail order catalog. I know the story well enough, but without the words "Boots Story" on my index card under that section of the outline, I risk forgetting to tell it. Also, speaker notes help you give a presentation in a more natural, conversational style. That's because you are talking to people instead of reading to them. It is no accident that Microsoft PowerPoint has a feature that allows you to create speaker notes to accompany each slide. The team who designed PowerPoint obviously understood the advantages of having a good set of speaker notes.

For several reasons, I am not a fan of writing out your speech and reading it to the audience. First, when the audience knows you are reading word for word, many of them think that it is a waste of time for them to be in the room. If you are reading a document word for word, why not just give out the document and let them read it on their own? Second, reading from a script results in a stiff, formal, stilted manner of presentation that usually leads to boredom and disinterest among your listeners.

To be fair, in a few instances I have attended lectures where I knew the speaker was reading his speech word for word but was able to pull it off. In one case, the speaker was a gifted writer, and the talk was so well written, it was a pleasure to hear, even though he was only a mediocre speaker. In the other case, the opposite was true: The writing was just okay, but the speaker was a great reader, as some people are.

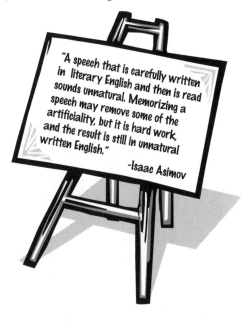

"A speech that is carefully written in literary English and then is read sounds unnatural. Memorizing a speech may remove some of the artificiality, but it is hard work, and the result is still in unnatural written English."

-Isaac Asimov

Off-the-cuff speaking should be strictly off limits for new and inexperienced speakers. It's usually not a good idea for even seasoned speakers. The only speakers who should ever attempt to give off-the-cuff talks are those with excellent memories. The late Isaac Asimov was one; he apparently had a marvelous memory and was also a comfortable, natural speaker with a great sense of humor. Speaking off the cuff or from speaker's notes, as opposed to reading from a text or reciting a script from memory, results in a more natural-sounding talk. Said Asimov, "If you speak off the cuff, you can speak colloquially, and you can easily shift moods and emotions to suit the reaction of the audience."

I am able to speak off the cuff on a number of my topics, but I prefer to have speaker notes because of the prompts (e.g., "Boots Story"). The prompts help me make sure I don't omit a story I want to tell. Without prompts, the mental concentration I apply to remembering what I want to say may detract from my performance. When I do give an off-the-cuff talk, I grab a piece of paper and quickly jot a few points and prompts to keep me on track before I take the stage.

Speechwriting Basics

For the novice speaker, one sensible approach is to first write out the full speech word for word. Then, from that full text, also prepare a set of speaker notes. Bring both with you to the podium. If you are feeling confident and competent, speak from your notes. If your confidence wanes, or you want to make sure to deliver a segment of your speech exactly as you wrote it, switch to the full script.

Writing for the printed page and writing for speech are different. Body language, voice tone, and facial expressions can be interpreted along with the words that are being spoken. Written text doesn't have these additional components, and lacks the ability to convey emotion and emphasis the way speaking does.

The average rate of standard speech in the U.S., from slow talkers to fast talkers, is 100 to 150 words per minute. When you write your speeches, you may want to figure on a rate of about 120 words per minute (including brief pauses for effect, laughter, or applause).

In every speech, there is a core message to be conveyed. You need to stick with this core message and build your talk around it for your presentation to be memorable and effective. What is your core message? What message do you want to get across to the listener? Tailor the speech to achieve that goal.

If you are writing a speech to be delivered by someone else, often the speaker will have trouble eloquently explaining what that message should be; this is where you step in to help them. Ask the speaker questions about the message. Offer suggestions that capture what they want to say. Ask the speaker to provide their idea of the message in one sentence.

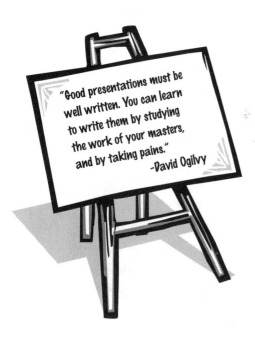

"Good presentations must be well written. You can learn to write them by studying the work of your masters, and by taking pains."
-David Ogilvy

Speakers are not limited to voice, words, tone, and gestures. Most amateur speakers fail to take advantage of interactive and three-dimensional media or to appeal to all five senses in their talks. Enhancements and aides need not be elaborate. Years ago, I taught a seminar on telephone selling. My prop was a plastic toy phone I borrowed from my kids, who were then preschoolers. When you hit a button on the phone, it rang loudly. During the workshop, I would have members of the audience practice cold calling, with me playing the prospect. When they dialed, I'd hit the ring tone, and then bring the phone to my ear. It enhanced the effectiveness of the exercise, making it seem more real, and also got a laugh the first time I used it during the session.

Keep the audience interested from start to finish. A series of audio, visual, and even oral devices can be used. Silence, for example, is a speaking technique. If your audience is noisy and won't settle down or stop talking, stand at the front of the stage, staring out into the crowd, and remain totally silent. They will quickly notice you, shut up, and take a seat.

Tailor your information to keep the audience interested in finding out about the message the speaker has to deliver. You don't need to get cute with the information you are trying to provide people. Unless you are writing a presentation to be delivered at an astrophysics or engineering conference, then you probably don't need to get overly technical. You can usually make a complicated message clear by using basic examples the average person understands. That's a big part of successful speeches.

Tell stories in the speeches you write and give. By this I don't mean in the literal sense of a short story or fable, but personal or relevant anecdotes. A story should have a beginning, middle, and an end. People like stories, and if you can involve people in the overall story, then you are going to have a successful speech.

Determining Length

Length is entirely dependent upon what the speaker needs you for. As you gain experience, you can suggest standard times for different speeches, from past speeches you have written. The length of a speech can vary between two to three minutes for a wedding speech, or it can be 20 to 30 minutes in the case of a corporate speech at a conference or other event. A training seminar can be a day or longer. Standard lengths are summarized on page 66.

UK-based speechwriter Brian Jenner said, "I am surprised by the number of people that want to speak for 10 or 15 minutes." He chose to use the example of the lyrics of songs—usually only three or four minutes—to illustrate how quickly you can impart a message, create emotion, and leave an impact on people. Ultimately, you will be guided in length by three things: the information that needs to be covered, the time you have allotted to speak, and your ability to convey your message in a succinct, to-the-point fashion.

The Crowd

Who are you writing for? Who is going to be in the audience? This is an important aspect of speechwriting. To use a parallel example, most newspapers are written in 7th grade English so they can appeal to a wide demographic. They cater to the audience they are trying to reach.

You need to apply the same approach to the audience you or your speaker is trying to reach. For a simple example, say there are two crowds—one consisting of parents and the other high school teens. The context will have to be decidedly different for each group. The message may be the same (e.g., the music program is being cut for lack of budget); however, how that message is conveyed to each audience will be different.

The Message

Say your speech will be ten minutes on tourism in your county for the local Elks Club. Simple and straightforward. As the speaker, what you need to focus on is the message, as it is the foundation of your entire speech. Everything else you say should tie into the core of the speech.

The message is the final impression, belief, attitude, or fact you want to leave the audience—the one thing you want them to remember or "get" if they remember or get nothing else. Say you are trying to help them understand the importance of tourism and how their support for a new electronic message board will help direct tourists to the different community events. OK, there is the message in long form. In short form, the core of this message might simply be: "We need funding for an electronic sign." Simple enough for them to understand. As long as everything you say brings them back to the message of funding, then you have taken the first step. Now you need to show them why their funding is going to help bring tourists into the county. Stick to the message.

Five Elements to Support the Core Message

Here are five weapons in the speaker's arsenal that can help you get your core message across to your listeners. Each one of these builds on your core, and makes the message more believable and more effective:

1. *Statistics.*

2. *Examples.*

3. *Credibility.*

4. *Humor.*

5. *Stories and anecdotes.*

Verifiable statistics can make the information more credible. Statistics can also be used to reinforce the statements you are making. For instance, in their mail order fruit catalog, Harry & David make their Royal Riviera pears sound like a rare and exclusive gourmet treat, noting: "Not one person in a thousand has ever tasted them." Sounds great, but another way of interpreting that figure is that hardly anyone buys them and they are not popular. McDonald's used to take the opposite approach with signs for its hamburgers advertising "over one billion sold."

Examples are one of the most valuable tools in creating impact in many speeches. Use examples your audience can relate to. In a financial seminar aimed at blue collar investors, the speaker told the true story of how a mill worker who never made more than $11 an hour was able to donate $2 million to local colleges—money he amassed not through an inheritance, winning the lottery, or by earning a high salary, but through careful investing.

Statistics and examples both add to the credibility of your speech, but giving that a hand is the injection of real world credibility. If your speaker is

THE BREATH TEST
To make sure a sentence is not too long, read it aloud at a moderate speaking pace. If you run out of breath before you get to the end of the sentence, it's too long. Break into two or more shorter sentences.

lecturing about a new natural health supplement but hasn't tried it, there is no credibility. If the speaker uses it religiously, and they have gotten over 2,000 others to use it, this adds credibility to the information. Sy Sperling, founder of the Hair Club for Men, a company selling hair replacement systems, was its most credible spokesperson and best salesman because Sy used his own product. Perhaps you remember his famous line: "I'm not only the Hair Club President; I'm also a client."

Humor is a powerful tool when used correctly. Humor should rarely be directed at anyone but the speaker—and never to a segment of the population or the crowd—if it could be interpreted in a derogatory manner. Humor serves to break the ice with the audience and can open them up to the purpose of your message.

Stories and anecdotes are another arrow in the speaker's quiver. People like to hear how something has affected people like you and me. Stories are how information has been shared for centuries—and it is an effective tool to use in a speech. Just make sure the stories stick to the message of the speech and reinforce what you are trying to convey to the audience.

Keep It Simple

Your audience has a much easier time digesting the message when you make it simple. Use simple facts, stories, analogies, and words. It's not dumbing down the speech down; it is just making it clear and easy for people to grasp.

Why do so many speakers fail to keep it simple? Two reasons: First, they want to impress the audience with how smart they are and how much they know. But you are there to express, not to impress. Second, writing and speaking simply takes work. It does not come naturally to many people, and they are unwilling to put in the work necessary to make every point clear.

Specifics Sell

The best way to make a message stick and sell your ideas, recommendations, or methods to your audience is to be specific. As the legendary advertising man Claude Hopkins wrote in his book *Scientific Advertising* (Bell, 1923): "Generalities roll off the human understanding like water off a duck's back." If you include more than just the dry description, people latch on to what you are saying. They remember those parts of the speech. So surround your most important elements of the speech with details. Use details, when needed, to help illustrate your message in a way that people can understand. Use details to help break down complicated concepts into simple ones.

For example, if you say, "After the accident, it was a long recovery time," it achieves the purpose of describing that you were in an accident and you were seriously injured. But it's more memorable when your description is a bit more detailed and specific: "I remember one of the few moments I was able to open my eyes and see what was going on around me, the flight nurse from the rescue helicopter was saying to one of the other nurses, 'We have to get him to the ER right away. I don't think he is going to live.' And then I closed my eyes, not knowing if I was going to ever wake up." Deliver that statement in a speech about drinking and driving to a group of high school students just prior to their graduation night, and you'll have their attention.

The Three Parts of Your Speech

A good speech has three separate parts: the beginning, the middle, and the end. Why? You want the speech to be a story of some sort. I use the term loosely, but it should have the beginning, middle, and end, like every good story.

The beginning, middle, and end are all important. But the beginning and ending are in some ways more important than the body. Most people can manage to discuss a topic for fifteen minutes, give a list of facts, or read from a prepared statement. And that's what it takes to deliver the middle part. The beginning and ending are a bit more difficult to master.

The Beginning

The beginning or opening of your talk—say, the first five minutes or so—must perform, in a very brief space, three important functions:

1. Establish rapport and a connection with the audience.

2. Communicate what the talk is about.

3. Explain why the content is important or useful to the listener.

In the beginning, people are going to want to know what the speech is about and why it is important. So that's what you do. It can be through example, statistic, or anecdote; it doesn't matter. You just need to get this across to the people you are speaking to. Stick to the core message when you are in your beginning. The audience should be able to identify what your core message is (or close to it) from the beginning of the speech.

In doing this, you must immediately engage the audience's attention *and* establish rapport. Not only must audience members be made to feel that your topic will be interesting, but they must be drawn to you, or at least not find fault with your personality. To test this theory, a well-known speaker put aside his usual opening and instead spoke for five minutes about himself—how successful he was, how much money he made, how in demand he was as a speaker, why he was the right choice to address the group. After his talk, he casually asked a member, "What were you thinking when I said that?" The man politely replied, "I was thinking what a blowhard you are."

How do you begin a talk? One easy and proven technique is to get the audience involved by asking questions. For example, if addressing telecommunications engineers, you might ask: "How many of you manage a UNIX data center? How many of you also have desktops that run on Microsoft? How about Sun Microsystems?" If you are speaking on a health topic, you might ask, "How many of you exercised today before coming here? How many of you plan to exercise after the meeting tonight? How many of you exercise three or more times a week?"

Asking questions like these has three benefits. First, it provides a quick survey of audience concerns, interests, and levels of involvement, allowing you to tailor your talk to their needs on the spot. Second, it forces the audience to become immediately involved. After all, when you are in the audience, and the speaker asks a question, you do one of two things—you either raise your hand or you don't. Either way you are responding, thinking, and getting

Take Notes

Here is a standard opening, given to me by motivational speaker Rob Gilbert, that you can use if you are stuck for a beginning.

When [MEETING PLANNER] was putting this session together on [TOPIC], she thought, "Who do I know who is the top expert on [TOPIC]?" So she called and asked that person to give the talk, but he told her, "I'm sorry, but I can't."

A few weeks later, she still hadn't found a speaker, so she said to herself, "I can't get the topic expert, so I'll get the person who is the best speaker." So she called and asked that person to give the talk, but he told her, "I'm sorry, but I can't."

Now she was getting desperate. She said, "I can't get the top expert, or the best speaker, so I will just get the best looking person I know. But—you guessed it: When she called and asked that person to give the talk, he told her, "I'm sorry, but I can't."

So I'm sitting in my office a few weeks ago. The phone rang and it was [MEETING PLANNER]. She said, "We are having a conference and I need someone to speak on [TOPIC], and you came to mind as the perfect speaker for the job. Will you do it?" And I said to myself: "I can't say no to her four times in a row."

involved. Third, it allows attendees to let others know something about them; people like being the center of attention, if only for the millisecond it takes to raise their hand and be counted.

I said earlier that you should speak from notes and not memorize or read your speech. But I do recommend that beginning speakers memorize the opening 60 to 90 seconds of their talk. The reason? Until you speak many times and become comfortable giving presentations, your anxiety may build rapidly just before you are about to start. When you have the opening minute or so written, rehearsed, and nailed solid, it helps eliminate this anxiety.

If your opening does nothing else, it should (at minimum) help you establish rapport with the audience. If people like you, you are halfway to achieving your goal, whether it's to sell your product, get their buy-in to your proposal, or motivate them to improve their performance. "Likeability may well be the deciding factor in every competition you'll ever enter," writes Tim Sanders in his book *The Likeability Factor* (Crown Publishers, 2005). "The more likeable you are, the more likely you are to be on the receiving end of a positive choice from which you can profit."

The Middle

The middle of your speech is the longest section. It is the main body; the "meat" of your talk. All talks are a long middle bracketed by a short introduction on the front end and a short ending on the back end.

The middle contains all of the information that you need to get across to the audience. It should stick to the core message as well; however, you do have a little bit more latitude here than with your beginning, because you may have other objectives you need to meet in this portion. I like to think of the middle as the part that ties the beginning and the end together. Not because the two need to be tied together, but it acts as a natural bridge to help the story along. The key to writing the middle of your talk is to choose a sensible scheme for organizing your content; if you need guidance on this, go back and reread Chapter 3.

The End

The end is going to make the beginning and middle make sense. You can call it the crescendo, the culmination, the final words—whatever. But it should be the point when you sum up everything and make everyone nod their head, clap their hands, or cheer, because they understand what you are trying to say.

Understanding how all of this goes together is the key to making your speechwriting successful. This is how the foundation of your speech is built. Always remember to stick with the core message and weave your words around that. Make it interesting, keep people's attention, and most of all, make sure they leave your space with the message.

While the beginning is important, don't neglect a strong closing, especially if you are there not just for the pleasure of speaking but to help promote your company or its products.

Your closing should be a call to action, though that action doesn't always have to be literal and immediate. If you simply want the people in your audience to mull over your ideas, tell them this is what you want them to do or think about doing.

Although you want a great opening that builds rapport and gets people to listen, and an ending that helps "close the sale," don't neglect the body or middle of your talk. It's the "meat"—what your audience came to hear. If your talk is primarily informational, be sure to give inside information on the latest trends, techniques, and product developments. If it's motivational, be enthusiastic and convince your listeners that they *can* lose weight, make money investing in real estate, or stop smoking.

If your talk is a how-to presentation, make sure you've written it so your audience walks away with lots of practical ideas and suggestions. As actor and Toastmaster George Jessel observed, "Above all, the successful speaker is sincerely interested in telling his audience something they want to know."

When speaking to technical audiences, tailor the content to listeners' expertise. Being too complex can bore a lot of people. But being too simplis-

Take Notes

"Speakers, as you now know, are also in the selling business, and the conclusion is the time to ask for the order. Nothing will happen if you don't ask. And you ask by telling the audience what you want it to do with the information you've presented and how they can take that action. An effective speaker presenting a central idea ends by pointing out to those in his audience exactly what is needed from them to put that idea to work. For example . . . if you've been persuading them to give blood, tell them where. And make it sound easy to get there."

-Dorothy Leeds, *PowerSpeak*

tic or basic can be even more offensive to an audience of knowledgeable industry experts.

Researching Your Talk

In today's information age, the information you need is often found at the touch of your mouse pointer. While the library, expert interviews, academic information, and other sources are always important, much of what you need can be found on the internet.

In fact, you can type in most questions into the Google search engine, and it will come up with an answer of some sort—or at least direct you to where you can find the information. Becoming a savvy searcher is the key to tapping into the vast amount of information on the internet.

Make sure the source of your information is credible in itself. A blog run by an anonymous stranger making a claim about cancer treatment does not have the same credibility as an article from a peer-reviewed medical journal. Some of the information on the internet will actually contradict other sources—so you should check facts in your presentation to make sure you aren't saying something that isn't quite true or can be challenged by an audience member.

When conducting a search through vertical search engines or a certain category in a directory, you naturally narrow the search. A search through the broad-based engines, on the other hand, may lead to a lot of wasted time on irrelevant sites.

For instance, although the query "Picture of DNA" resulted in numerous hits with some of the search engines, that doesn't present a problem, since the needed information was within the first or second page of the search results, regardless of the search engine used. However, when your desired site is hidden on page 38 of the results, you spend too much time searching. In other words, the search engine can return a lot of "noise"—non-consequential results.

So, how can you narrow the search? You can do it either on the main search bar, or by using the convenient, ready-made templates identified as the "advanced search" feature. The "advanced search" option is offered by all the major search engines.

Much of database searching is based on the principles of Boolean logic. First discussed by the British born, Irish mathematician George Boole (1815-1864), these are logical ways to formulate precise queries using true-false connectors or "operators" between concepts. This is a mathematical system that is used today for queries on the World Wide Web, and is designed to produce better search results. Sounds complicated? It really isn't. See Appendix VI for a detail on how to use Boolean operators to fine-tune your web searching.

Once you've reached a web page through the search engine, find the search terms in order to judge their relevancy. Pressing "Ctrl F" brings up a "find" template for the searched word or phrase. This works for most web pages. In most PDF files, the "find" template is already at the top of the document when read with the updated version of Adobe Reader (which is a free program, available at adobe.com/products/acrobat/readstep2.html). If the "find" template is not at the top just press "Ctrl F". This is an invaluable time-saver feature!

Optimizing Information Density

"Information density" refers to the ratio of content (facts, data, tips, ideas) to total verbiage, and in terms of an oral presentation, this means the number of new facts, ideas, or supporting data points covered per minute.

In the old days, before the internet, the challenge of the speechwriter was to conduct enough research. The difficulty was finding sufficient supporting facts and data to prove the point the speaker was making.

Today, in the internet age, we have the opposite problem. Facts are easy to find, not only for the speechwriter or speaker, but for everyone else. A mistake you want to avoid is feeling you must include a fact in your presentation just because it's interesting, or just because you found it at all.

While the typical speech is supposed to be informative and educational, that doesn't mean you cram the speech with every fact and figure you can find. If the information density is too high, your audience becomes over-loaded. They can't follow your presentation. They can't extract or remember the core message, which is lost in a maze of data and references. Worse, they become bored.

An old rule of thumb for speakers who use audiovisual aids is one slide per minute. Since each slide communicates one key idea, this suggests an information density of one new fact, tactic, or strategy per minute. If your presentation is communicating ideas that need to be explained, elaborated on, or made clear through examples, anecdotes, or exercises, your informa-tion density might be considerably less than that. In a 20 to 30-minute speech after lunch or dinner at a club meeting, I find I can cover 7 to 12 points. For a 60-minute presentation at a conference breakout session, anywhere from 10 to 25 points can be comfortably covered.

Keep Things Moving With Entertaining Stories

We talked earlier about using anecdotes in your presentations. There are a few ways to acquire good stories and integrate them into your presentation.

The best source of stories is things that happen to you, either those that directly relate to your topic or those that are just good stories. People absolutely love stories. When you are speaking, if you sense energy waning in the room and attention flagging, insert an interesting and relevant story between content points. Personal stories are best. For one thing, they are yours, so the audience hasn't heard them before. The audience relates to them more because the subject of the story—you—is right in the room with them. Because they are personal, you can deliver the story with genuine emotion (but don't overdo it).

Everyone who is alive today has good stories to tell; stories that are interesting and that illustrate a point, move people, educate, inform, or motivate. You tell stories all the time when you talk to people. Funny things, inspiring things, sad things, and tragic things happen to us all.

The second source of stories is things that happen to others. These may be people you know personally or anecdotes you've read or heard. Get in the habit of reading a daily newspaper; they are filled with dramatic stories you can clip from the paper, file for reference, and incorporate into your presentations.

Is it OK to make up stories? I would avoid pure fabrication unless you say in advance that it is not a real story. I think it's OK to tell a story about someone who is a composite of several real people, but again, only if you identify it as such before the telling.

A third source of stories is books. You can get stories from your reading. There are also a number of books of anecdotes, some written specifically for use by professional writers and speakers in their articles and talks. I would caution you against filling your talks with stories you get from speaker reference books. Many of them are old chestnuts that are fast becoming clichés or at least com-

Stories Get Your Point Across

Stories and statistics can both be effective in presentations, but stories are by far more powerful. Reason: Statistics appeal to logic, while stories tap into emotion.

"If a newspaper reports the sad story of a youngster dying of cancer and how the family is planning an early Christmas for him, letters, money, and gifts will come to them from perfect strangers," says speechwriter Joe Kelley. "People sympathize with and are saddened by the plight of an individual. A few columns away from that story, an item may report the deaths of 10,000 in a flood in India; it will be scanned and passed over."

ball. You also risk repeating a story the listeners have heard from other speakers who also have the same anecdote reference book on their shelves.

I also caution you against lifting stories from other speakers you hear, for the same reason. Many people have heard these speakers, and may recognize that you have presented their anecdote as your own. The repetition makes your talk less interested and unoriginal, and audiences lose respect for speakers they feel do not present original material.

Borrowing vs. Stealing Material From Other Sources

There is an old joke about speakers who steal material from other speakers. The joke is the first time they use the purloined joke or anecdote, they attribute it to the speaker from whom they heard it. The second time, they say it is not original to them, but conveniently "forget" where they got it and fail to identify the source. After that, they use the material freely with no acknowledgment, as if it were their own—and they may have even convinced themselves that it is!

My rule of thumb for using material from other sources—whether a story taken from another speaker's lecture or the results of a research study conducted at a university—is to always give attribution to the source. First, it's the ethical thing to do. And second, you protect yourself against being accused of plagiarism.

Having said that, what can you safely borrow and what should be original to you? As much as possible, make the core message and content of your speech your own ideas, research, experiences, stories, strategies, techniques, and knowledge. Doing so enables you to deliver unique value other speakers can't. If your talk is merely bits and pieces from stuff you have heard and read, then your audience can just go read those books and listen to those tapes; they don't need to get a recycled version from you.

Incorporating Humor Into Your Talks

Jokes are easy enough to find. You hear jokes all the time, and if you want to use jokes in your talk, be sure to write down the ones you like and keep them in a reference file labeled "jokes." Appendix VII lists a website where you can access hundreds of jokes online. And there are many joke books available in bookstores.

Adding humor to your presentation is generally a good idea. "I found in my life in advertising that if you could get clients to laugh, they usually bought your ideas," says Michael Gates Gill in his book *How Starbucks Saved My Life*. But you must realistically evaluate whether you have the ability to tell a joke in a way that seems natural instead of forced and gets a laugh.

The safest way to incorporate humor into your presentations is to avoid jokes unless you know yourself to be a very good joke teller. Otherwise, spontaneous, good-natured, and self-effacing humor works best. As mentioned earlier, do not make fun of or put down anyone in the audience or anyone else for that matter, except yourself. Here's an example of how I used self-effacing humor (that was also unplanned) to great effect. As it happens, I am a bit overweight and stocky. At a conference, the speaker before me was a ripcord thin personal trainer who proudly announced that he had only 8 percent body fat. When he stepped off the stage and I stepped onto it, the first thing I said to the audience was: "I too have only 8 percent body fat … *in my little finger.*" The crowd ate it up. Another reason why self-effacing humor works so well is that people don't like speakers who are egotistical or brag in any way. Using humor that pokes fun at you as the target makes you seem humble, human, personable, and likeable.

If you are comfortable acting spontaneously and adlibbing, this can add humor to your talk in a more natural way than forcing yourself to tell a joke you head from someone else. Once during a talk, the instant I paused between points, someone's digital wristwatch alarm went off with a persistent beeping at a loud volume. It took him several seconds to find the switch to turn it off. All eyes were on him, and he was embarrassed. When he finally silenced it, I paused another second and said, "Time to take my medicine" in a deadpan voice. To this day I don't know exactly why I said it other than it was the first thing that popped into my head. I have a pretty good instinct for what will make people laugh, and it did.

Stopping Your Listener From Nodding Off

No matter how dynamic or entertaining a speaker you are, there will be times when you sense the energy in the room fading and the audience's attention waning. It may be your fault. It may be that you are speaking to a group who was forced to attend; e.g., high school students sent to an auditorium to hear an anti-drug speaker, or company employees taking a training class they don't want to attend. Or you may be scheduled to speak after a big lunch has been served or as the last speaker of the day at a resort where everyone wants to leave early to have cocktails.

There are several techniques you can use to get your presentation back on track and energize the audience enough to last to the end. One is called a "pattern interruption." This means that you wake up the crowd with a change in their pattern. For instance, if they have been listening to straight lectures all day, get them to do a group exercise or game.

Here's one you can use: During or immediately after a break, before you start speaking, say to the audience, "Let's get the blood flowing. Would you stand up please?" When they stand up, tell them to turn and face the wall on their right. Next, tell them to put their hands on the shoulders of the person in front of them—and then, to give that person a good rubdown! This almost always gets a laugh and brings the energy back into the room (the only two groups it doesn't seem to work well with are engineers and accountants).

Here's another pattern interruption I use in my talks, and this one actually has a point. I tell them to stand up and reach as high as they can. Once they have done so, I tell them to now reach even higher. Most are puzzled. A few stand on tiptoes. Finally, one person figures it out; they step onto their chair or table, and then reach up. The point this supports is that by thinking outside of the box, or by putting in a little more effort, we can always do better than we think we can do.

Reference the Familiar

A technique that can add interest to your talk and grab the audience's attention is to reference current events; things that are going on in their lives or

Take Notes

In his book *The Electric Life of Michael Faraday* (Walker & Company, 2006), Alan Hirshfeld quotes Michael Faraday, a great scientist who was also one of the most popular lecturers of his day, on using local and current references in your talks:

'Tis well too when a Lecturer has the ready wit and the presence of mind to turn any casual circumstance to an illumination of his subject. Any particular circumstance that has become table talk for the town, any local advantages or disadvantages, any trivial circumstance that may arise in company give great force to illustrations aptly drawn from them and please the audience highly as they conceive they perfectly understand them."

their work right now. The event can be national, such as the rising price of a gallon of gasoline at the pumps. Or it can be a local reference, such as a road construction project that's making commuting difficult in their town because it is going on far too long.

One warning: Stay away from controversial subject matter. Religion and politics are the two universally controversial topics that should be avoided. On a local level, steer clear of any controversial or unpopular topic that might turn the audience against you, which could be anything from the debate over a new leash law to recycling. Subjects that are virtually always safe to reference include sports, movies, and the weather.

CHAPTER 5

The Visuals

> "Visuals help keep your prospects' attention from wandering and reinforce what you're saying. Research has shown that any point is far more likely to be remembered if it is heard and seen."
>
> – Bruce J. Bloom

In the old days, most orators stood at the platform and captivated crowds using nothing more than the power of their voice. But not the scientist Michael Faraday, who became one of the most popular lecturers of his day; he gave lectures explaining science to the general public and demonstrated each principle with an experiment he performed as he spoke.

According to presentations coach Terry Smith, visuals can:

- help people remember
- keep things organized
- save time
- add emphasis
- aid understanding
- provide focus
- gain attention
- add fun and enjoyment.

Making Audio and Visuals Work Together

One of the biggest mistakes made by people giving speeches that use multi-media props is that they simply regurgitate the information that is on each slide. Does the speaker not realize that the audience is fully capable of reading what is on the screen? Maybe not.

The most successful speeches use visual aids not for show or as a crutch, but as a springboard to get the core message across and illustrate the supporting points. This is the concrete portion of the speech. The facts, figures, and charts on the screen reinforce and illuminate the message that is being spoken. You have no doubt heard the expression about one picture being worth a thousand words. Well, in a speech, your time is limited. So visuals can convey extra information you don't have time to fully present. With the ability to show concepts and facts that support and expand the core message of the speech, you don't have to waste time covering that in your speech.

The use of multimedia is to emphasize, illuminate, and illustrate the message the speaker wants to deliver or its supporting facts. Your visuals hold the supporting material for the core message including statistics, examples, credibility, charts, graphs, and pictures. A number of presentation systems are available for presenting your visuals to your audience. These include:

■ *PowerPoint*. Despite the tendency of speakers to misuse or overuse PowerPoint, and the proliferation of boring presentations it has spawned, PowerPoint has become the de facto standard for presentation visuals. One reason is the tendency of Microsoft products to become the industry standard in their category; e.g., Windows in PC operating systems, Word in word processing, SharePoint in collaborative applications. Another is that PowerPoint is included as part of the Microsoft Office suite. Also, PowerPoint presentations are easier to use than many of the media below. They are portable; you can carry them on a CD or your laptop. And you can deliver them to meeting planners in seconds as an attachment to an e-mail.

Flip Chart Tip

In a flip chart presentation, if you don't want the
audience to read the next chart until you flip over
the current one, leave a blank page or two between
them. Charts written in black or other bold colors
show through a single covering sheet, but two sheets
keep the page hidden until you are ready to show it.

■ *Flip charts.* These can be helpful in a situation where a PowerPoint presentation is not an option. They serve a similar purpose. "Post flip charts
with key points," write Matthea Marquart and Alexa Sorden in an article in *Training and Development* magazine (4/07, p. 26). "By writing the
points out, the facilitator will ensure that they are covered in the correct order and with the appropriate language." I like flip charts because,
as with a blackboard, you can write on them. This allows you to create visuals "on the fly" to emphasis or capture ideas. Unlike
PowerPoint, which only shows one slide at a time in full size, each flip
chart can be torn off the pad and taped to the wall for simultaneously
display of multiple visuals.

■ *Video.* Video can be used to help instruct, to illustrate, or emphasize
key points, and it can be used within the context of the PowerPoint
presentation itself—or as a standalone feature. Video is extremely effective at engaging the audience attention in a society where the average
American watches over four hours of television every day. The growing popularity of YouTube and other social networking websites has
caused a resurgence in video viewing, especially online. According to
a February 2006 *New York Times* interview with Julie Supan, YouTube's
marketing director, YouTube had more than 10 million videos viewed

daily. "We're streaming 115 videos a second," she said, "6,944 per minute." According to eMarketer, 123 million Americans view an on line video at least once a month. That's a massive amount of video viewing, and the trend is continuing to grow.

■ *Audio*. Audio is neglected in favor of video, but I have used it to great effect; e.g., when I gave seminars on cold calling, I played tapes of actual cold calls I had recorded, which the class listened to and then critiqued in group discussion. Dr. W. Proctor Harvey, the nation's most skilled practitioner of auscultation—the ability of a doctor to detect cardiac illness by listening to a patient's heart sounds—played classical music records in his medical school lectures. The purpose: Teach medical students to recognize sounds by properly identifying the different instruments they heard on the recordings.

■ *Overhead transparencies*. The overhead projector is still used in situations where your speaker needs to present information, though it is considered old technology and used only infrequently today. One advantage of overheads is that you can prepare them in advance as well as write additional material on them with markers during your talk. You can also cover overhead transparencies with a sheet of paper to gradually reveal the text or visuals on them bit by bit. There are a couple of drawbacks to using overheads, though. For one thing, the plastic sheets tend to cling together, making it a bit tricky to place them on and remove them from the projector and each other. Also, when you drop them, they can easily get out of order. Unlike 35 mm slides, overhead transparencies cannot be organized in a tray or other holder.

■ *White boards*. Use bright, bold markers on a white board to write down suggestions in an interactive speech or to help illustrate the information you are trying to get across to the audience. In a room with pull-down screens or where the white boards can be closed and covered, you can write out presentation points in advance, and then reveal them in sequence as you get to each segment; this prevents the audience from reading ahead and knowing what's coming. Make sure the markers you have been supplied are specifically for white boards. If you use the wrong marker, it dries instantly, is extremely difficult to erase, and may even ruin the board.

Making Presentations and Speeches Mesh

Here are three ways you can integrate your visuals into your presentation:

1. *Visuals as prompts.* The information on a slide or chart that is provided should be used as a prompt to speak the message. Don't say the same thing; use the information as a prompt for something you can say to move the entire speech along. Normally, the title and bullet points in each slide are my prompt. Occasionally, I want a prompt for myself without letting the audience know what is coming. You can do this by printing out a hard copy of your slides, marking some private notes with a pen, and keeping this hard copy in front of you on the podium. Or, you can print coded prompts directly on the slides in small type; e.g., "PDS" for "purple dog story." If anyone asks, and they almost never do, I just say it's a note to remind myself to cover a certain point.

2. *Present the Big Picture.* The big information—big numbers, big statistics, big flow chart, big process diagram, big schematic—can be put into a presentation. Helping people understand what this information means, and how it relates to the core message is the responsibility of the speaker. The slides you use in your presentation contain the important detailed information that you will explain in your talk. When I am teaching a process, I like one of my early slides to be a flow diagram (see page 98) showing the sequence of steps in that process. This immediately gives the audience a view of the "big picture"—the total process I am about to teach and break down for them.

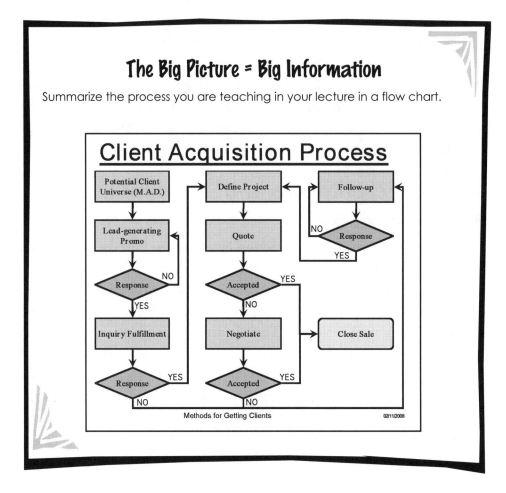

3. *Quick transitions.* You need the speech to move along with the visuals or the other way around. Don't let the audiovisual part of your presentation slow the speech down or the overall effect is going to lose steam. Keep the transitions quick, so the speech doesn't get bogged down. If you are waiting for slides and it disrupts the speech, you could lose some of the audience members. The slides and your speech should be in synch; you don't want to spend 17 minutes on one slide, then 30 seconds on another slide. Pace your presentation more evenly. Reason: If you have been spending one minute per slide, and then you have a slide that you're going to talk

about for 15 minutes, the audience becomes impatient for you to move to the next slide. Do not say to the audience, "There's a lot of information on this slide, so I will give you a minute to read it," and then stand there in silence waiting for them to do so. If the slide is too lengthy or complex for them to digest while you are talking about it, shorten and simplify the slide until it communicates the point at a glance, or spread the information over several slides.

Presentations Using PowerPoint

In today's technological age, the increasing reliance on computers has infiltrated the speechwriting industry. It seems that the boardrooms and conferences are littered with laptop computers that are perceived to be more effective than the speaking themselves. Still, at some point you will be asked to tailor a speech to a PowerPoint presentation. No problem. With the knowledge you have already gained in this book, you should be able to use the PowerPoint tool to achieve many of the elements you need to support the core message.

Here are some more tips for creating winning PowerPoint presentations:

1. Simplify the slides and use key phrases and necessary information.

2. Use contrasting colors between the background and the text. Don't use overly dark backgrounds; when you print the presentation, your slides will be difficult to read and it will also waste a lot of ink.

3. Make good use of "white space" so the text is easily readable and the viewer can separate each point.

4. A good rule of thumb is one slide per minute of presentation in a steady linear progression; constantly flipping from slide to slide can be a bit of a distraction, especially for people who cannot read the slide as fast as others. If you need to refer to a slide more than once, insert it each time it comes up in your talk. Don't worry about the repetition. It's better than flipping back and forth, which is distracting.

5. Keep the slides consistent. Don't vary the design of each slide by using different colors and fonts from slide to slide. Stick with a simple and clean presentation. Don't go color, font, and picture wild, importing images and graphics simply because they're there and you can.

6. Avoid the temptation to over-use "fly-in" and other special effect transitions that PowerPoint provides. These can limit the impact of the overall speech and PowerPoint presentation. You may be taken with the novelty of such techniques, but they are usually nothing more than window dressing. Audiences usually interpret an over-designed and over-produced audiovisual presentation as way of compensating for poor content or a lousy talk.

7. Make sure you know how to operate PowerPoint to go backward and forward on the presentation when required. If required, it should be easy to go back to an earlier slide for further discussion.

8. Don't speak to the slides, speak to the audience. Look at the audience, not the projection screen or your laptop. Don't read from the slides word for word either. You have the PowerPoint presentation for the audience, not for you to dictate from. A quick glance for cues to elaborate on the slide is just fine.

9. Avoid excessive punctuation, and refrain from using the ALL CAPS feature when producing slides. If you want emphasis, emphasize in your speech, rather than on the screen. You may occasionally use large type or other graphic devices for emphasis, but do so sparingly. Overuse of any such technique reduces its effectiveness.

10. View the presentation ahead of time from various points in the room. You want attendees watching from all angles and distances to be able to clearly see the message on the PowerPoint presentation.

11. Use the information in the PowerPoint presentation to reinforce what you are saying. For example, say the core message of your speech is to show

employees of a corporation the effect of day-to-day changes they have made in their operations. On the screen, a slide comes up that shows a graph illustrating a sharp increase in profit over last year. You say: "We have increased electronic communication between departments, we have reduced costs by buying in bulk, we have increased productivity through bonuses, and you can clearly see the effect it has had on our corporation's bottom line. You should be commended on your efforts." The PowerPoint slide shows a bar chart or graph indicating how each of these variables has increased or decreased as you said. This reinforces the message, and rings loud and clear with the employees.

12. Avoid using cute pictures, clever visuals, or beautifully decorated slides that detract from the overall message. You don't need pictures of flowers, fast cars, and smiling, happy people—unless your speech deals with flowers, fast cars, or happy people.

Run through the speech several times using the slides. Timing is essential when you are coordinating an audiovisual presentation with a speech. The audience will remember a major foul-up more than they are going to remember the message, so avoid this at all costs.

Unfortunately, even though you run through the presentation numerous times, you still may encounter a technical glitch—with the computer you are using or with the AV equipment. Make sure you know how to use the computer in case of a glitch with the system. Time is ticking and the audience is getting restless in their seats if they have to wait too long for problems to be fixed.

If the computer or AV equipment decides to take a nosedive, it could leave the speaker and his or her audience hanging if not handled effectively. If the speaker is alone without an assistant to handle AV, then it might just be best to continue the speech without the aid of the AV prop.

If you have someone assisting with this AV aspect of the presentation, the assistant may be able to quietly iron out the problem and seamlessly slide back into the presentation. If that doesn't work, it is usually just best to leave the AV alone, rather than cause a big fuss over the material.

Be careful not to overuse the gadgetry in a speech. Reliance on the audio and special effect features could prove to be more of a distraction than an attraction for the presentation.

Common PowerPoint Mistakes and How to Avoid Them

As discussed, PowerPoint has become the standard tool for presentation graphics. While PowerPoint can be made rich in complexity and design, the key to an effective PowerPoint is keeping it simple. When I was a marketing communications representative at Westinghouse in the late 1970s, slides were all the rage in the corporate world. Nearly every presentation was an audiovisual presentation. Two managers literally could not get together for an informal chat without one pulling out a slide projector and dimming the lights.

Slides are still popular today, especially PowerPoint, but in my opinion, audiovisual aids are not always necessary. Many professional speakers—people who earn thousands for a brief talk—do *not* use audiovisual aids. I feel that business people, especially in the corporate world, become overly dependent on the visuals and lose the spontaneity and relaxed manner that come with "having a conversation" rather than "making a presentation."

The problem with the common corporate approach to being dependant on visuals is that the audiovisual aid is seen as something that must run continuously and concurrently with the talk. So, although only 10 percent of the presentation requires visuals, the slide projector runs for 100 percent of the time, and the speaker fills in with stupid "word slides" that are wasteful and

Practice Makes Perfect PowerPoint

PowerPoint slides that look good on the PC sometimes don't work well in an actual presentation. Solution: Be sure to practice aloud with your PowerPoint slides. If a slide doesn't fit in well with the flow of your talk, or isn't clear, or takes too long to work through, you'll spot it instantly. For slides that take too long to explain, you can often divide the information over multiple slides, so you don't spend too much time on a single, dense slide.

silly. For instance, if the speaker is going to talk for three or four minutes on quality, she hits a button, and the word QUALITY appears on the screen in white against a black background. Such a visual adds nothing to the talk and is, in fact, ridiculous.

A better approach is to have visuals you can use when appropriate, and then deliver the rest of your talk unaided. When I speak, I sometimes use flip charts and markers instead of or in addition to PowerPoint. In some cases, I don't prepare the flip charts in advance. Rather, I draw as I speak, which adds excitement and motion. It also creates anticipation; the audience becomes curious about what is being created before their eyes.

Slide projectors, LCD projectors, and even laptop computers can experience mechanical failure. Errors in presentations, such as difficulty sorting through a pile of overhead transparencies, or slides that are upside down or out of order, or a laptop with a graphics card to weak to project the PowerPoint presentation on the conference screen, confuse and embarrass the speaker; they also cause the audience to snicker or lose interest.

I have seen speakers who, interrupted by a jammed slide tray, lose their train of thought and never fully recover. Errors or mishaps with audiovisual support can be extremely disconcerting, especially when making a good impression is important or the presenter is not comfortable with public speaking in the first place.

At times, high-quality visuals are needed to demonstrate how a product works, explain a process, show the components or parts of a system, or graphically depict performance, perhaps. For instance, if you are trying to promote your landscape design practice by giving a talk entitled "How to Design a Beautiful Front Yard," you want to show pictures of attractive front yards you have designed. If your speech is entitled "Advancing Science Using Supercomputer Generated Images," people will want to see color slides of those images.

In such cases, I suggest you prepare PowerPoint, overhead transparencies, a videotape, flip charts, or similar displays that can be shown for a brief period and then turned off for a bit. If you use slides, turn the projector off and the lights up when the visuals are not in use.

According to a research study from 3M, it's estimated that we retain only 10 percent of what we hear; by adding visual aids, the retention rate increases to 50 percent. And a report from Matrix Computer Graphics notes that 85 percent of all information stored in the brain is received visually.

Actually, I'm not convinced they're right. I can recall a number of memorable presentations—the speaker, the delivery, and many of the ideas—but I can't recall a single slide or visual from those talks. But then again, I am an auditory and reading learner. For visual learners, the slides may indeed be more valuable.

If you do use PowerPoint slides, make them bold, bright, colorful, easy to read, and not too cluttered. Slides and overheads are used to show, demonstrate, and create excitement. They are not a good medium for transmitting complex detail.

CHAPTER 6

Involvement and Interactivity

"Involve your audience.
Ask questions and
wait for answers.
Ask for a show of hands."
- Alan Sharpe

Thanks to computers, TV, and the internet, audiences have short attention spans and are easily bored by straight lecture. The successful public speaker knows communication is a two-way street and actively engages the audience using a variety of techniques.

No speaker succeeds by boring the audience. And one of the most boring things to your audience is monotony; more and more of the same thing. You have of course heard the saying about variety being the spice of life. Well, variety can also help spice up your talk and keep monotony at bay. The longer the talk, the more critical variety becomes. You can get away with lecturing non-stop for a 20-minute luncheon talk, but it's boring for a full hour, and for a full day— absolutely deadly.

The most effective way to add variety to a lecture is audience involvement and interactivity. When the audience is actively involved in the presentation, it increases their interest and attention. They participate more, learn more, retain what they have learned better (because the event is more memorable), and give higher ratings both to the instructor and the presentation (evaluation forms often ask attendees to rate the instructor, the presentation, and sometimes the audiovisual and the handouts separately).

Internet marketer and speaker Joel Christopher calls his weekend workshops "Funshops." I like that title, because it correctly acknowledges that, in addition to learning, the attendees want to have fun. When people come to hear you speak, they just don't want a dry lecture or recitation of facts. They want to:

- Learn the latest information and techniques.

- Get practical, actionable strategies they can take back home and put immediately to work.

Engaging Your Audience

"Why would anyone listen to a speaker instead of daydream? Authenticity. When an audience member can tell that what they're hearing isn't canned, hasn't been said exactly the same way to multiple groups, they are more likely to listen. So although preparation is key to giving strong presentations, it's also essential to make sure there's life in your presentations. One way to do that is to integrate a short interactive portion into your presentation. You can ask attendees to answer a question or to ask a question or to do an exercise and then share it with the group. It takes practice to do this well, to basically improvise on the spot, but it makes for much livelier presentations."

—Ilise Benun, professional speaker

- Be entertained and enjoy the learning experience.

- Feel that the value received from the workshop was far in excess of the time and money spent to attend it.

- Connect with others in a similar situation, share common experiences, exchange ideas and experiences with their peers, and add new contacts to their network.

- Have fun and maybe even laugh a little.

- Believe that the speaker is not just there to pick up a check from the meeting planner, but cares about the audience and wants to help them succeed.

Adding interaction and involvement to your presentation can help your students enjoy these experiences and get the most out of your talk.

Pre-Workshop Speaker/Audience Bonding

In any presentation of two hours or longer, for groups of 30 people or fewer, I like to have some sort of exercise at the beginning to help bring the audience and the speaker together. A great tool for doing this is an Audience Affinity form.

On the master of your Audience Affinity form, you create a grid. In each box on the grid, you type an activity, interest, or characteristic that the people in your audience are likely to have; e.g., have taken their kids to Disney World, enjoy Mexican food, ski or snowboard, watch *The Simpsons*. You can customize an Audience Affinity form to your subject and audiences, or use the generic form found in Appendix V.

At the beginning of the program, you hand out the form, and explain to the group you want to help everyone get to know each other a bit better. For the next five minutes, everyone moves quickly from one attendee to another, asking that person if they fit any of the boxes on the form. When you find someone who has done the activity, you put a check mark in that box. The first person who completes the form is the winner, and gets some prize; I offer three of my hardcover books with a total retail value of over $60.

I've used this Audience Affinity Audit several times. People enjoy it, and so do I. It's fun to see people get animated, run around the room, hustle to get their form completed first so they win the prize. Each person has, of course, done a number of the items on the grid themselves. So as they identify others in the group who have done or like something they have done or like, an instant connection is made. This principle of finding common ground improves your ability to make friends and influence people whether you are giving a lecture, meeting new people in a social situation, or cold calling a prospect on the phone. People like people who are similar to them and share their interests. By finding a common bond, you forge an instant connection and get the other person to like you.

Transforming an Audience into a Team

When giving corporate training programs, the attendees may be from separate departments and divisions. But more often, they all work in the same area or group. In either situation, your client—either the manager who supervises all these attendees, the training director, or a human resources manager—always has "getting his people to work as a team" as an ongoing priority.

A seminar or workshop is not merely an opportunity to learn a specific skills or body of information, but also to build fellowship and cooperation among the attendees. I have met people at conferences and workshops I've attended who I still keep in touch with to this day, and I have a few students from my workshops I still hear from 10 or even 20 years after they attended my class.

The most obvious way to get people working as a team is through group exercises, which we will discuss in a bit more detail below. The speaker divides the attendees into equal size groups. The groups are then asked to solve a problem or work on an exercise. In a seminar on branding, for instance, groups of marketing managers, brand managers, and product managers might be tasked with coming up for a slogan or positioning statement for a new product.

There are companies that specialize in team-building exercises; e.g., several bring executive teams into the woods for survival weekends. On a less intense level, company softball and bowling leagues also help build teams. One of the simplest team-building exercises is a treasure hunt. You plant one or more objectives in the room or area, and give out a treasure map or clues.

Sy Sperling, founder of the Hair Club for Men, made it a priority in business to share a meal with the people he dealt with. He felt that "breaking bread"—having lunch or dinner—gave him an opportunity to really know the other person. You have the same opportunity when giving a lecture. At a conference, don't hide in your room or escape from the hotel for a break; take your meals with the attendees. Attend their other functions during your stay. In corporate training sessions, suggest that the meeting planner bring lunch into the room for the attendees. This saves time and allows you to get to know them better. If you are speaking at a corporation, conference, or meeting over several days, and the meeting planner asks if you are available to have dinner with her and some of the attendees, accept graciously, and enjoy yourself. You will gain additional background on the group and their challenges. They will get to know you on a more personal level. Both of these things can help make your program an even greater success.

Individual, Small Group, and Large Group Exercises

In my half-day and longer workshops, I like to use a mix of individual, small group, and large group exercises. Let's use my writing seminars as examples. Since writing is a skill gained through practice, my seminar involves heavy use of exercises. Each exercise fits on a single side of an 8½ by 11-inch sheet of

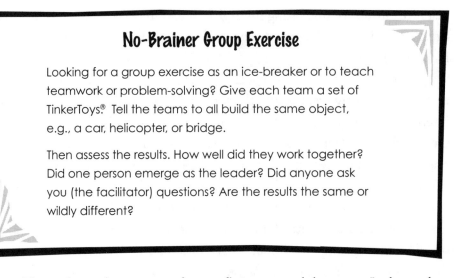

No-Brainer Group Exercise

Looking for a group exercise as an ice-breaker or to teach teamwork or problem-solving? Give each team a set of TinkerToys.® Tell the teams to all build the same object, e.g., a car, helicopter, or bridge.

Then assess the results. How well did they work together? Did one person emerge as the leader? Did anyone ask you (the facilitator) questions? Are the results the same or wildly different?

paper. This reduces the amount of paper flying around the room. It also makes the exercise brief enough to finish in a reasonable amount of time.

For most of my individual writing exercises, I give the class about five minutes to work on it before we review the results. In one exercise, I may give them a sheet of paper with some writing that is not punctuated, and ask them to punctuate it correctly. Or I may give them a sheet with two columns; on the left are big words, on the right are simpler substitutes. I ask them to match each big word with its correct substitute. Once they finish, we review the answers. I make the exercises short enough that most people can finish in five minutes. And I make them simple enough that most attendees will get about 80 percent of the answers correct. If an exercise is too easy, and they get all the answers right in a minute, the class feels you are really not teaching them anything new. If they struggle to get any right, it's too difficult and they will become frustrated.

After starting off with an individual exercise or two, I change the pace by doing a small group exercise. In small group exercises, the speaker divides the class evenly into groups, who work on the exercise together; ideal group size is usually three to five members. Because groups discuss ideas, argue points, and must reach consensus, group exercises take five to ten minutes. After the exercise is complete, a spokesperson from each group stands up and summarizes their recommendation, answer, or suggestion. In my workshop, "How to Write Ad Copy That Sells," I give the attendees a sheet with a description of a product; the groups are asked to come up with headlines for an advertisement selling that product.

In a full-day seminar, I typically do several individual exercises and maybe two or three small group exercises. I also like to do one exercise that the entire class does together. One of my writing exercises utilizes a handout with a list of redundant phrases; I go around the room, and ask each attendee to rewrite one of the redundant phrases to eliminate the redundancy (e.g., changing "armed gunmen" to "gunmen").

The Keeper of the Time

As another involvement device, at the beginning of the seminar, I ask one member of the group to be my timekeeper. I tell this person they have to alert me to what time it is on the hour and every half hour, by saying the word "time." The purpose of this is to keep me on track. I further tell the person that they are required to shout out the word "time" in "a loud and obnoxious manner." My classes have tremendous fun with this, helping the timekeeper to figure out creative ways to carry out her task. In one class, they loaded up a Super Soaker water rifle and, when the half hour rolled around, the timekeeper sprayed me with water. Everyone was laughing, and as I've said, when people are laughing and having a good time, they are more receptive to your message. More details on how I use the timekeeper are given in Chapter 8.

The Socratic Method of Teaching

Perhaps the oldest form of student interaction is the Socratic method of teaching. In the Socratic method of teaching, instead of just revealing the information, the teacher asks questions. The students then attempt to answer the questions, in discussions led by the instructor. By answering questions instead of just listening to a lecture, the students are forced to reason out the answers on their own, instead of being spoon fed the information by the teacher. As a rule, the Socratic method of teaching can help the students master the material faster and on a deeper level than when the seminar leader does all the talking. But be careful, as overuse of the Socratic method of teaching can become monotonous. It can also compromise the instructor's authority, as some students conclude that the instructor is asking them for the answers because he does not know the answers himself.

Using Props

In a seminar setting, a *prop* is any object used as a presentation aid. For some topics, the props can and should be directly related to the subject matter; e.g., a high school science teacher performs experiments on his lab desk to illustrate or prove the chemical laws he is teaching. In other cases, the props are not directly related to the topic, but a clever speaker can find a way to tie the prop in with his theme or message. For instance, my friend David Yale was giving a talk on direct marketing. From a magic shop, he purchased as a prop a magic wallet. When you open the wallet, you hear the pop of a small explosion, and you see a spark and then smoke come out of the wallet, which obviously is rigged with a small chemical charge. "The point," said David after performing the trick, "is that without knowing these direct marketing principles, your profits can go up in smoke." Chapter 8 contains additional suggestions for incorporating props effectively into your presentations.

Games and Contests

Games and contests are another form of interactivity that can liven up a seminar and get the audience actively involved. One example is the Affinity Audit Form we discussed earlier. But you can use whatever strikes your fancy; there are so many games you can play; the choice is limited only by your own imagination. For instance, I happen to have a great storehouse of pop culture trivia in my memory (I actually wrote five published trivia books). So when an attendee brings up a pop culture subject, I break in with a spontaneous short trivia quiz. Often it has nothing to do with the seminar, but it gets the group energized, thinking, and engaged. Another group activity you can use to get juices flowing is mild physical exercise, like stretching in place. In one workshop I attended, the instructor gave everyone a supply of soft foam rubber balls. She explained that one of the rules of the workshop was to respond to ideas with specific criticism or suggestions for improvement; you were not allowed to say merely "I don't like it." If you did, other people in the room

were invited to throw the balls at you to chastise you for your breach of the rules. It generated a lot of laughter and maintained a high level of energy in the room throughout the day.

Prizes and Rewards

People love to win things and get stuff for free. So if you can incorporate that into your event, it can get your audience excited and enthusiastic. I attended a presentation on print advertising at a marketing convention. The talk was given by the publisher of a magazine everyone in the room wanted to advertise in. The publisher had a fish bowl in the room. Anyone who attended his talk could enter a drawing by dropping their business card into the bowl. The winner got a free quarter-page ad in his magazine—a prize worth over $2,000.

Google expert Perry Marshall offered a free laptop computer to everyone who attended his first internet marketing boot camp. Terry C. Smith has a creative variation on this prize theme. He tells people in his seminar that they may walk away with a prize worth as much as $1 million. Naturally, everyone becomes eager to find out how to win the prize and what it is. It turns out the prizes are small sealed envelopes. In each is a lottery ticket with a million-dollar potential payoff. No one resents that Terry is not actually giving away a million dollars in cash, because no one in his right mind would expect that. They think his prizes are clever and enjoy getting them.

Shockers

A "shocker" is something done, presented, or taking place during the seminar that is totally unexpected. Some possible shockers include:

- An appearance by an unannounced celebrity or guest expert.

- An invitation to attend a follow-up workshop at a deep discount or free of charge.

- An unadvertised bonus—a free book, free CD, free DVD, or other free training materials.

- A drawing for a valuable prize—e.g., a free private consultation with the speaker.

- An unexpected act of generosity on the part of the speaker or meeting planner—e.g., picking a student to partner with the speaker on a project.

- An unplanned dinner in a good local restaurant, paid for by the sponsor.

Once, I was giving a talk on how to make money as a freelance writer. At the end of my talk I said, "I really want you to succeed in this. So if you have any questions, call or e-mail me any time." A student raised his hand "How long is that offer good for?" he asked. "For life," I answered, causing the crowd to gasp with astonishment. "Of course," I added, "that's my lifetime, not yours."

I have heard of wealthy businesspeople speaking to classes of underprivileged high school seniors about the importance of doing well in school, and then offering to pay the full cost of four years of college tuition for any students in the auditorium who graduate with good grades. Was it planned or spontaneous? I don't know, but it certainly came across as spontaneous. My offer of lifetime help for my seminar attendees was likewise unplanned.

In an internet marketing workshop led by Joel Christopher, he gave the students an unexpected bonus: a master copy of one of his other workshops on DVD, with unlimited rights to resell it as their own product, with no royalty or commission payment to Joel. For many of the students, this gave them an instant product with which to launch their internet marketing business. I don't know if any of the other attendees did anything with that gift; I suspect they did not. But I did; I repackaged it and sold it as a product, and have made thousands of dollars in revenues from it so far.

Many speakers hesitate to make free offers to their attendees for fear they will be overwhelmed with requests. But here's a little secret known by almost all experienced speakers: Almost no one will take advantage of whatever extra free service you offer them. In my technical writing workshops, I offered 30 days of free e-mail support—attendees could e-mail me documents and I would review and edit them at no extra cost. The 30 days of free online support was included in the price the corporate sponsor paid for the training segment. Often, when negotiating a presentation with a corporate client, mentioning the 30 days of free online support would help convince them to hire me. Ironically, almost no one ever used this service. If after teaching a technical writing class with 25 engineers I would be sent one document to look at within 30 days, I'd be shocked. What happens is that you make the offer, but people are busy. So they promptly forget about the extra support, and the overwhelming majority never take advantage of it.

Shockers work because people like surprises. Of course, it has to be a *pleasant* surprise; the shocker can't be anything bad. Offering to critique the attendee's work or give advice for free after the class is over is a pleasant surprise, even if they never use the service. Telling students they are going to have to attend another day of class tomorrow because their boss thinks they need extra help or giving them big homework assignments is not a pleasant surprise.

Humor and Fun

As you can see if you've read this far, I am a speaker who likes to inject a lot of humor into my talks and have a lot of fun with the audience. Doing so is easy for me because it comes naturally; in school I was a clown. In addition, I am fairly quick on my feet and what pops into my head and comes out of my mouth tends to be funny.

If you are a naturally somber person, you may not want to emulate my approach. But you should strive to make your seminars fun to attend. Nothing can destroy your effectiveness as a speaker or lower your evaluations faster than being boring. If you lack a sense of humor, people will find you boring. You don't have to tell jokes to be funny, though it's not a bad idea to memorize a couple of strong jokes and be able to tell them well.

Very few people in the world have absolutely no sense of humor or enjoy being with those who have none. If you cannot get comfortable telling

---

Make 'em Laugh

Recently I attended a talk by Phil Rubin, an expert in customer service, who told a great story that got a big laugh from the audience:

A woman went to confession. She told the priest, "I met Brad Pitt on my vacation, and we had a night of passionate love-making." The priest tells the woman to say three Hail Mary's. "But father," she replies, "I'm Jewish." "Then why are you telling me this?" the priest asks. "Father," the woman replies, "I'm telling everybody."

I forget the point he was making with the story, though it did have one. But my point is that humor is a trait almost universally appreciated and admired.

---

jokes—and it's my belief that almost anyone can, with practice—then there are all sorts of other sources from which humor can spring. As Vernon Howard writes in his book *Talking to an Audience* (Sterling Publishing, 1963), "Anything that brings a laugh or smile to your audience is always welcome.

I like to play off real-life incidents in my sessions. In one seminar I was teaching, the meeting planner brought in gourmet ice cream bars as the afternoon snack. As I reached for one, one of the attendees good-naturedly asked me, "Concave or convex?" meaning did I have a stomach that protruded (convex) or was indented (concave)? I paused, took a noisy breath, sucked in my gut, smiled, and said "Concave!" Then I took a big bite of the ice cream bar, simultaneously pushing my stomach out, looked down, and said, "Oops—I guess convex!" Self-effacing humor always works, and it won me the group's affection.

Breaks

People have always had limited attention spans; in the internet age, their attention spans are even shorter. Only college students are willing to sit through a 90-minute or two-hour lecture these days. With adult learners, you should never go longer than an hour without at least a short break. In some situations, the meeting planner determines length and duration of breaks; in other cases, the seminar leader controls the breaks. Here are the types of breaks you can use to divide your seminar into short, manageable segments:

- *Stretch-in-place breaks.* Attendees stand and stretch in place without leaving the room or their place in it.

- *Two-minute beverage break.* Tell the attendees that coffee, water, and soda are in the back of the room and if they need a beverage, they can go back and grab one but must immediately return to their seats.

- *Five-minute human needs break.* Attendees can leave the room to go to the bathroom, make a phone call, get messages, or check their e-mail, but they must be back in five minutes.

■ *Long break.* This is a 10- to 15-minute break between major segments of the seminar.

■ *Lunch break.* This meal break lasts between 30 and 60 minutes; at some conferences, it can go as long as 90 minutes, especially if it is advertised as a networking lunch break.

See the table below for the frequency and length of breaks you should have during your talk.

Frequency and Duration of Seminar Breaks

Seminar length	Frequency and Type of Breaks
20 to 30-minute lunch or dinner speech	None
60-minutes keynote	None
90-minute breakout session or workshop	One stretch-in-place break halfway through
Half-day seminar	Beverage break after first hour, human needs break after second hour, human needs or beverage break after third hour
Full-day seminar	Start: 8 A.M. Stretch-in-place break: 9 A.M Beverage break: 10 A.M Human needs break: 11 A.M Lunch: noon to 1 P.M Beverage break: 2 P.M Long break: 3 P.M Human needs break: 4 P.M End: 5 P.M

Pattern Interruptions

In Chapter 4, we talked about "pattern interruptions." This means that you wake up the crowd with a change in their pattern. Just about everything in this chapter is a pattern interruption of one kind or another.

Remember, monotony is boring. Next to inaccuracy (wrong information) or offensiveness (being politically incorrect, insulting an attendee), being boring is the greatest sin a speaker can commit. Use pattern interruptions to change the pace, break the monotony, and snap attendees out of lethargy and indifference.

Don't cram more information into your talk
than your audience can digest.

CHAPTER 7

Getting Ready for the Big Day

> "Have you spent as much time in preparation and rehearsal as the audience will spend collectively listening to you?"
>
> —Terry Smith

Professional speakers often practice a single presentation dozens or hundreds of times before giving the talk at a fee-paid engagement. Even if you are not a professional speaker, your audience expects you to be practiced and polished.

"Practice and tape yourself," advises Mark Amtower, a talented speaker and expert on marketing to the federal government. "Listen to the tape to see if you like how you sound. Most of us don't the first time. If you have a monotone, re-record and use enthusiasm."

"Practice your presentation," advises advertising executive Bruce J. Bloom. "The last thing you want to do is stumble your way through. Start using your presentation only when you know it cold."

How to Practice by Yourself—And Not Feel Silly

When I first began speaking, I felt like an idiot practicing my talk out loud when my wife or anyone else was around. So I would get in the car, drive to my nearby office, and practice there. As long as I knew no one could hear me, I was fine. So find someplace—the attic, basement, the garage—where you can rehearse without prying eyes and ears on you.

When you rehearse, you have to do it at the pace and volume you intend to use when you actually deliver the talk in front of a live audience. When you are alone, you will be tempted to rush, or hurry through it, thinking it's just practice and doesn't count. But it does count, a fact you will discover when you finally take the stage. So treat your practice sessions as real. Do everything you would do if in front of an audience. That includes using your PowerPoint presentation and your props, and speaking at full volume and normal pace.

Getting Your Presentation Critiqued

Once you have practiced sufficiently to feel you are ready to give your talk in public, you want to have it critiqued, preferably by at least two parties: you and at least one other person whose judgment you trust. To critique yourself, you must record and listen to your talk on audiotape or watch it on video. To have someone else critique it, you must deliver the talk in front of him or her live.

Who should you choose to critique you? The ideal reviewer is someone who is much like the people who will be in your audience. For highly technical topics, you may want to give the draft of your speech or the speaker notes to a subject matter expert for vetting. For critiques of the presentation itself and of you as a speaker, here's a list of what the reviewer should look for and comment on.

1. Was the content clear and understandable?

2. Was it written at the right level for the intended audience?

3. Did the speaker maintain good eye contact with the audience?

4. Was the content useful and practical?

5. Did the speaker tell you not just what to do, but how to do it (or at least where to find out how to do it)?

6. Were the points covered actionable—ideas the audience can take back to the office and put to work immediately?

7. How was the pace of the presentation—too fast, too slow, just right?

8. Did the speaker articulate well? Did his or her voice project so that everyone in the room could easily hear him?

9. Could everyone in the room, including those in the rear row, easily read the slides?

10. Did the presentation match the expectations of the meeting planner and the attendees? Did the speaker cover all the points in his outline?

11. How well did the speaker relate to the listener? Did he or she adjust the content and delivery on the fly based on audience reaction and feedback?

12. Did the speaker come across as personable, likeable, and caring?

13. If you had taken half a day away from the office and paid $100 to hear the speech, would it have been worth the time and money?

14. Would you be eager to hear another presentation from this speaker?

15. Would you recommend the person as a possible speaker to meeting planners in your company or trade association?

Find Opportunities for Dry Runs

As I mentioned in the introduction, most people don't like public speaking and avoid it at any cost. But if you are serious about improving as a speaker, you want to do just the opposite. Volunteer to facilitate meetings, chair a committee, lead workshops, present training classes, give talks at the clubs you belong to. Practicing in solitude or with a colleague in the room can help you improve. But you get better much faster when you practice in front of a live audience. Obviously, your first forays into public speaking should be for smaller groups, noncritical talks, topics with which you are already familiar, and short formats. Start off with giving simple five- and ten-minute presentations. Practice until your comfort level is high and your performance improves. Then tackle more difficult speaking assignments of greater complexity, bigger challenge, and longer duration.

When to Stop Rehearsing

My experience is that the quality of anything improves as a function of time spent. Specifically, the greatest improvement comes with the early efforts. A person who has taken a year of piano lessons is light years ahead of someone who has taken only one lesson, and a person who has taken five years of lessons is many times better than someone who has taken only five weeks of lessons, given an equal amount of native talent and concentration during practice.

However, the more time you put into it, the slower your rate of improvement. If you record a serious amateur pianist after 10 years of lessons and again after 11 years of lessons, and listen to both recording, the difference may be very slight or even (to the untrained ear) undetectable.

Speaking follows the same curve; you make your greatest gains between giving your first talk and giving your tenth talk. As you gain experience, the incremental improvement per hour of practice slows. So let's say you have written a new speech. When can you stop practicing and feel you have gotten "good enough" at it?

My answer is in the figure on page 125. Most people stop practicing at point A on the graph. And it's too early. With a little more effort, they can go on to point B or C, still gaining a big improvement in quality worth the extra time required. However, beyond point C, you earn diminishing returns. The tiny incremental improvements are so minor they are not detectable to your audience, and are therefore not worth the time it costs you to achieve them.

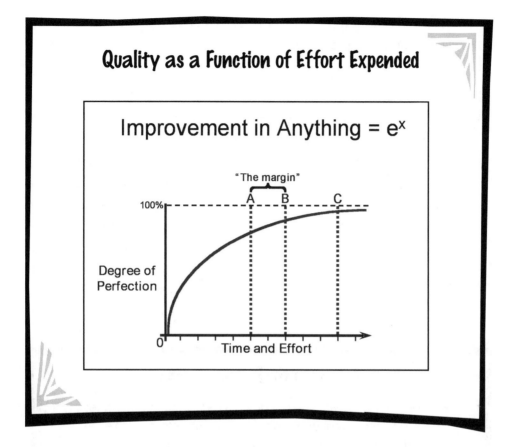

The Seven Worst Speaker Mistakes

I've given hundreds of talks, many of which I listened to later on audio cassettes or watched on DVDs, and I've sat through presentations by hundreds of other speakers. With all that experience, here are the most common mistakes I see speakers making, from the businessperson who has to give an occasional talk to his colleagues at work, to CEOs lecturing at major industry events, to professional speakers and seminar leaders:

1. *Total dependence on mechanical aids.* When a speaker is thrown off track because of a jammed slide projector or PowerPoint presentation that

crashed and cannot recover, the attendees hold him in disdain, lose interest, and stop paying attention.

2. *Failure to research the audience.* I knew a speaker who began his talks by saying, "I'm so happy to be here at the annual meeting of the International Cattleman's Association" when he was addressing other groups. It was a joke, and it got a laugh, but it raised an important point: A speaker who is not focused on his audience, and has not done his homework to learn their needs or concerns, is doing his meeting planners and audiences a disservice. Worse, if they figure out he doesn't really understand who he is talking to, they'll turn hostile quickly. For example, I attended a breakout session at the national meeting of the BMA, an association of business-to-business marketers. The speaker's presentation was packed with slide after slide showing different ad campaigns, every one of which was for a consumer product. Finally, a disgusted audience member said,

Getting to the Podium On Time

Being late for a speech you are giving is a disaster. Not only does it set the audience against you and upset the meeting planner, but the added stress can adversely affect your performance.

Call the meeting planner the week before the presentation to get the exact location including name of facility, address, and room number. Ask the hotel to fax you driving directions or get the route from MapQuest.

Leave extra early. You never know what can happen. Recently, I gave a talk to a local company. As I drove to their offices, traffic halted. I tuned into the radio and found that an accident had shut down the highway. With a GPS in your car, you can easily find an alternate route as long as you have the correct address to enter.

"These are all consumer ads. Don't you have any business-to-business examples?" The speaker replied defensively, "Well, the principles are the same whether it's business or consumer." "No they're not," the attendee retorted. He then got up and stormed out of the room along with several other members who were equally disgusted by the speaker's failure to tailor the material to the audience.

3. *Unsupported opinions.* When you make claims, especially those that disagree with an audience belief or perception, you'd better be prepared to back it up with lots of research and facts. Do not assume they will take your word for it or bow to your wisdom because you are supposed to be an expert. With most audiences, that cuts no ice, and they aren't impressed by your fancy title, Ph.D., or the fact that you wrote a book. Today attendees can easily research, on the spot, facts that support their disagreement with you using their mobile devices and Google.

4. *Wrong facts.* Most of us are lazy, especially so when it comes to the more mundane aspects of writing and speaking including proofreading, research, and fact-checking. One of the most embarrassing situations for a speaker is to make a factual error in a presentation and have an audience member point it out on the spot. It's embarrassing enough that you made the mistake. But since you didn't even realize you had made it, your reaction is likely to be even more embarrassing. If you aren't sure whether you are right, your tendency is to argue with your critic. Resist the temptation. Instead, promise to check after the talk and get back to him either way. If you staunchly defend an erroneous statement, and either everyone in the audience knows you are wrong, or an attendee who Googles the question on his wireless laptop quickly proves you are wrong, your face will be red.

5. *Lack of audience involvement.* If you get up, lecture for an hour, turn around, and leave, your audience will be disappointed—even stunned. A good speaker involves the audience, engages their intellect, gets them

thinking, stimulates participation, and stays to answer questions. When communication is one-way only, you have failed your listeners.

6. *Speaking in a monotone.* Monotony is boring, and speaking in a monotone is monotonous. There's no excuse for it, especially when it's so easily avoided just by varying your pace and voice volume.

7. *Politically incorrect behavior.* You are not allowed to insult any member of the audience. You should not make statements about other people or other things they are likely to find insulting. This rule can be violated by political speakers and those who address social issues, but not by business speakers, seminar leaders, and keynoters.

Why You Should NOT Have a Professional Speaker Coach You

"It is the first rule of oratory that a man must appear such as he would persuade others to be; and that can be accomplished only by the force of his life."
—Jonathan Swift

Let me modify that statement a bit. I think working with a speaking coach is okay, provided that coach works mainly with business people who speak, rather than professional speakers for whom speaking is their main business. Why? A lot of speaking coaches who work with professional speakers focus on the theatrics of speaking; gestures, voice inflection and modulation, movement, and dramatic emphasis. They teach you to be a professional entertainer, an orator. The speakers they train develop affectations and a phony manner designed to create a false impression. Doing so negates everything that is unique and genuine about the speaker—the exact things that make you valuable and worth hearing. If you must work with a speaking coach, find one who works mainly with executives and entrepreneurs—

real people—and not professional speakers. Focus on correcting speaking defects (e.g., hesitation, mumbling, and difficulty being understood) and content (delivering a talk with solid information).

Audiences want you to be a good speaker with solid content. They will not readily forgive either a skilled speaker who has nothing of value to say to them or an inept and boring speaker who conveys a lot of information during his dry, dull talk. However, after the talk, they will grudgingly admit that the dull speaker gave them some useful ideas. But they will universally feel the glib speaker who delivered no practical content was an utter waste of time.

Toastmasters

I have never been a Toastmaster member, but I have attended a number of Toastmaster speaker competitions. Membership is something you may want to try, as there are a number of clear benefits:

- You regularly speak before a live audience to quickly accumulate the hours of practice you need to get better.

- You speak in a low-pressure environment where poor performance does not hurt your business or career.

- The competitions put strict time limits on the speakers (most talks are only a few minutes), which teaches you how to speak within the time allotted and not go over budget.

- You will see many speakers (your fellow members) perform, some good, some terrible—and you can learn a lot from both.

- The meetings are local and usually held in the evening so as not to interfere with school or your job.

- Winning one of the contests, even at the lowest level, will boost your confidence and give you a credential you can use as a boasting point in your speaker's bio.

■ Being a member communicates to your employer that you are serious about improving your ability to communicate, a skill executives value in those they hire and promote.

Videotape

We talked earlier about videotaping your presentations so you could watch yourself deliver your talk. Whenever a meeting planner will agree to it, encourage them to videotape your live performance in front of their group. Tell the meeting planner that you will allow them, at no cost, to distribute the video of your talk to their attendees and members in any manner they wish. They can give it away for free or sell it; burn it onto a DVD or post it as streaming video on their website. In return, you want a copy of the master. And, you also can do with the video whatever you wish. If you are a businessperson speaking to promote your company, you can post selections from the video of your speech on your company website or even on social networking sites such as YouTube. Increasingly, online videos are driving traffic to websites. Also, you can put a 10-minute excerpt from your talk on a CD and offer it as a demo to meeting planners who are thinking about having you address their group.

Other Public Speaking Aids and Resources

Some useful books, websites, and other resources for speakers are listed in the appendices. If you speak regularly, I recommend you attend at least a couple of seminars every year. Doing so lets you observe other speakers. Pay attention to their delivery, content, and presentation materials. Often you will pick up presentation methods and ideas you can adapt to your own speeches. Also, get in the habit of ordering tapes or CDs of the speakers at conferences you attend or even those you can't get to in person. The more speeches you hear, the more you advance in your own abilities as a public speaker.

CHAPTER 8

Delivering Your Presentation

The Secrets
of
Speaking Success

When I am on stage or at the front of the room and the meeting planner says "Now, let me turn it over to Bob," the waiting is over and it's show time. In this chapter, I'll share with you techniques for giving a great presentation whenever you're in front of a group, whether it's a handful of people sitting in someone's office or the keynote at a major national convention.

Overcoming Anxiety, Nervousness, and Stage Fright

According to an article in *Science Digest*, psychologists estimate that 80 percent of the population suffers from stage fright. What can you do to overcome butterflies? Practice helps. The more speaking experience you gain, the less frightening it seems. There are also seminars that teach stress relaxation and confidence-building techniques designed to reduce nervous tension.

However, many professional speakers would advise you not to eliminate *all* of your stage fright. A little anxiety, they say, is a good thing. It pumps you up, keeps you sharp and alert, and helps you "get psyched" so you can do your best.

There is a lot of cliché advice out there about overcoming butterflies. The most popular: "Picture the audience naked." I recently read an article that advocated having sex before you give a speech! The most effective antidotes for nervousness are much more mundane:

- Pick familiar topics, those that you already know inside and out.

- Prepare twice as much material as you think you have time to deliver. This eliminates one of the greatest speaking fears: Finishing your prepared comments early and having absolutely nothing else to say.

- Put the major points you want to make on a flip chart or in a slide you can refer to in case you get flustered and go off track.

- When you feel the need to mentally regroup, stop talking, deliberately and slowly pour yourself a glass of water, and take your time drinking it. This has a calming effect and gives you the time you need to recover in case you get lost or feel anxious.

- In half-day and longer workshops and training classes, whenever you feel the need for a break, hand out—and have the class work on—an exercise that takes at least five minutes. As soon as you hand it out and give instructions, leave the room. I either step into the hall, or go to the bathroom to wash my face, or take a short walk up and down the hall. If you want to step outside, be careful. I once had the door lock as it closed behind me, and barely got back into the building in time.

- Another good break for you as the instructor is to have a training video to show during your class. When you feel the need for a time-out, pop the DVD into the player. You can step into the hall, but stand near the door so you can make sure the video is play-ing without a problem and know when it is just about over.

- In half day and longer seminars, have the stu-dents take a short stretch break, bathroom break, water break, coffee break, soda break, or whatever every hour. If you tell them the break is for two to three minutes, they'll prob-ably be back in five minutes. I tell the class we will take a short "human needs break" every hour; this always gets a chuckle.

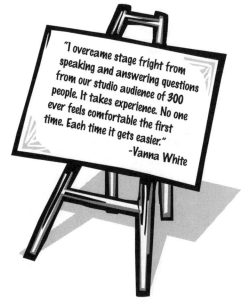

"I overcame stage fright from speaking and answering questions from our studio audience of 300 people. It takes experience. No one ever feels comfortable the first time. Each time it gets easier."
-Vanna White

- Remind yourself that the experience is finite. Even a full-day seminar will be over by the end of the day. If you are nervous, picture yourself relaxing in your car as you drive home after the event is over. Think about how good it will be to go outside in the fresh air after being inside a stuffy room giving a talk all day.

- Promise yourself a reward after you finish your presentation. When I speak in Washington, D.C. and then drive home to New Jersey, my reward is stopping at a rest stop on the Garden State Parkway and treat-ing myself either to Popeye's chicken or a pepperoni slice of Sbarro's pizza with a Coke.

The Secret for Speaking Success

Never talk about things you don't know. This is a good tip for public speak-ers, bloggers, writers, and anyone else who communicates. Stick to what you know and you'll be a more effective, more persuasive, more credible com-municator. And by "knowing" a thing, I don't mean just researching and read-ing about it. I mean knowing from actual experience. The only way to ensure

In Robert B. Parker's Spenser novel, Cold Service, Spenser says this to Susan about his sidekick, Hawk: "He's nearly always right. Not because he knows everything. But because he never talks about things he doesn't know."

total credibility as a speaker is to not speak on a subject unless you've actually done it. If you haven't done it and an audience member challenges you, you are completely vulnerable, because you don't totally know what you are talking about.

As discussed in Chapter 2, narrow the topic. One of the biggest mistakes speakers make is to try to cover too much material in too short a time. The result is a rushed presentation that is either superficial, because no point can be covered in any meaningful way; or one that is boring, because the information density is too high, and there is too much for the listeners to absorb. The solution is to narrow your topic.

In Chapter 3, we talked about the importance of properly organizing your material. One way to do this is to choose a title that dictates an organizational scheme to follow. If your title is "Safe Handling of Compressed Cylinder Gases in the Plant," you are then faced with deciding how to organize your content. On the other hand, the title "Ten Tips for Safe Handling of Compressed Cylinder Gases in the Plant" dictates that the content is organized as a series of 10 guidelines or suggestions. The "Ten Tips" in the title has the added bonus of making attendees look forward to the talk; they become curious, and want to know what the ten tips are.

Remember to use the 3 Ts Formula to frame your talk: Tell them what you're going to tell them, tell them, and then tell them what you told them. If you are using PowerPoint, insert a slide between your title slide and the first slide of the material that says, "What We Will Cover Today." Underneath that heading, list in bullets the main points to be covered on the remainder of the slides. After the last slide of content and before the closing slide (typically a logo, the speaker's contact information, or a call to action), insert a duplicate of the "What We Will Cover Today" slide with the exact same bullet points.

But change the heading on this second slide to read something like "What We Covered Today" or "To Sum It All Up." Go through that slide point by point to show how indeed you covered everything you promised you would. This is a sore point for many seminar attendees who complain that the presentation was not the one promised in the conference brochure, and that the speaker did not cover some of the topics the agenda said he would. When you demonstrate that you have covered what you said you would, the audience feels more satisfied.

Public speaking coach Terry C. Smith advises, "Have something worthwhile for the audience." In other words, show them how they will benefit from the advice or content in your talk. For instance, if your talk is announcing a new treatment for varicose veins, tell the audience some things they can do to prevent or relieve the symptoms of the condition—like mild exercise or wearing special stockings. I like to give my audience a simple, practical strategy or tip right up front, within the first few minutes. If you accept the premise that getting even one good idea makes the entire seminar worth attending, giving this tip early ensures the listeners that they have already gotten their money's worth, and the rest is just icing on the cake.

Avoid the well-meaning but misguided advice of speaking coaches and trainers who teach you theatrical techniques or tell you to change your

Rehearse!

Your presentation will never be great the first time you give it. So you want to give it many times before you're actually in front of your audience. That means rehearsing. You can rehearse by yourself or in front of your staff or family. Or, you can accept speaking gigs in venues that aren't critical to you (e.g., the local library or YMCA) before unveiling your talk to your target market—the people whose response really matters to you.

manner, voice, and posture. Just be yourself. Audiences respond much more positively to real people than to mannequins and phonies. Also, says Terry, "Keep telling yourself, 'I'm glad that I'm here, and I like what I'm doing'—even if it's a damn lie." If you are not happy to be there and you give in to that feeling, it will show in your talk. My experience is that even if you don't like giving talks and don't look forward to doing them, once you step up to the lectern and open your mouth, your distaste will vanish and you'll gain enthusiasm.

Work the Crowd

It is important to know your audience, since different people are interested in different aspects of a subject for different reasons. Let's say, for example, that the subject of your presentation is clean-in-place filtration. Engineers would be interested primarily in the capabilities of the available equipment, while plant operators would want to learn how the systems work and how to troubleshoot them. Purchasing managers, on the other hand, would be interested in their cost. Tailor the content you present to the problems, needs, concerns, fears, worries, and desires of the audience.

Seven Tips for Better Speeches

1. Show your connection to the place at which you're speaking.

2. Ask a key question and then answer it.

3. Give the audience a quiz.

4. Wow them with an amazing fact.

5. Throw one funny item into a list of serious points.

6. Tell a vivid story from your experience.

7. Start with something shocking.

—Philip Theibert, *How to Give a Damn Good Speech*

Spice Up Your Speech

Many businesspeople, when faced with giving a talk, do so with a minimum of preparation, perhaps because they feel that the topic is so cut and dried that a straightforward recitation of the facts is sufficient. But it isn't. If your voice drones in a monotone, or if your talk is dry, or if the content lacks excitement or new or useful information, your audience will be bored. And you will lose them early in the speech.

Technical topics are not dry and dull in themselves. Rather, whether a subject makes for an interesting talk or a boring one depends on the style of the speaker and the content of the lecture. Make your topic fascinating by digging for useful applications, immediate benefits, new developments, or little-known facts. Read popular science magazines, the better trade journals, and science stories in newspapers to see how skilled writers turn highly technical material into interesting reading, and employ these same techniques. If you need a clear explanation of a technical or scientific subject, get a children's book on the topic and read how the author explains it.

Be Prepared

How much time goes into researching, writing, and preparing for a speech? According to *Best Sermons,* a religious magazine, it takes clergymen about seven hours to prepare a 20-minute sermon. Terry Smith says that to give his best effort requires one hour of preparation for every minute he will talk. Of course, the time you must spend preparing your talk depends on several factors: Your experience and skill in public speaking; your technical knowledge of the topic; whether the assistance of a company technical writer or speechwriter is available; and the importance of the talk. Also, it takes considerably less time to brush up an old presentation than to create a new one. The point, however, is that preparing a memorable address requires many hours—much more time than inexperienced speakers ever dream would be required. Plan your schedule accordingly so you can give your talk the attention it deserves.

In a 20-minute, 2,400-word presentation, there are limits to the amount of information that can be transmitted. To ensure a meaningful, informative talk, focus on a narrow, specific subject rather than a broad-based area. For example, "Chemical Process Equipment" is too broad a topic for a presentation, but 20 minutes is just the right amount of time for giving a useful lecture on "Seven Tips for Sizing and Selecting Static Mixers."

Write for the Ear, Not the Eye

A speech is just that: speech. And writing a speech is not the same as writing for the printed page. Words intended to be spoken must sound like conversation, or else the talk will seem stiff and stilted. To ensure a good talk, read your rough draft aloud first to yourself, and then to others. Rewrite any sentences that sound awkward or unnatural until they roll off the tongue (and into the ear) smoothly and naturally.

Avoid lengthy sentences. The problem with an extremely long sentence is that by the time you get to the end, the listener may not remember the beginning, and so the ending doesn't make sense. For oral presentations, a good tool for evaluating sentence length is the breath test. Read your sentence aloud at a normal speaking pace without taking a deep breath before you start. If you run out of air before you get to the end, the sentence is too long. Solution: Break lengthy sentences into two or more shorter sentences. To do this, find a point in the sentence where a new idea begins, place a period after it, and make the next part a separate sentence.

A little humor can help lighten a heavy technical talk and prevent your audience from drifting off. But overdoing the humor can ruin an otherwise fine presentation and erode your credibility. The best way to handle this is to pepper your talk with tidbits of warm, gentle, good-natured humor. Be wary of using outright jokes, unless you are a natural-born comedian. Do not use off-color humor at any time, because what is funny to one person is offensive to another. Never lead off with a prepared joke. If it fails, it turns off the audience, and you look like a clown.

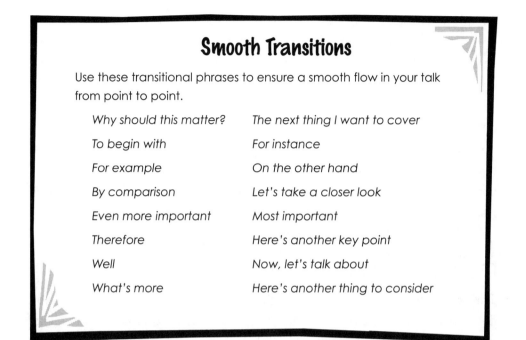

Smooth Transitions

Use these transitional phrases to ensure a smooth flow in your talk from point to point.

Why should this matter?	*The next thing I want to cover*
To begin with	*For instance*
For example	*On the other hand*
By comparison	*Let's take a closer look*
Even more important	*Most important*
Therefore	*Here's another key point*
Well	*Now, let's talk about*
What's more	*Here's another thing to consider*

Research Your Topic

You are probably knowledgeable about the topic of the presentation, or you wouldn't have been asked to talk. But this doesn't mean you know everything about it or even enough to put together an engaging lecture. Good speakers supplement their own knowledge and experience with outside research and examples. The library is an excellent place to start. Books, magazines, newspapers, trade publications, DVDs, and audio CDs can provide a wealth of data, ideas, advice, and anecdotes. Interviews, informal chats, and e-mails exchanged with colleagues and experts in the field can further add to this information. And, of course, there is a wealth of information on even the most arcane of technical subjects on the web including content-rich websites, articles located through a Google search, blogs, and forums.

Keep a file with hard copies of all your research materials. Clip and save newspaper and magazine article. Photocopy pages from books. Print out e-mails and articles from the web. Note the source of each, in case you are ever challenged. Today, if you lose a source document, you have a fighting chance of finding it again with Google. But why take the chance? Keep good research files for all your speeches.

Gather about twice as much material as you need. Then, when drawing on these data, you can be choosy, selecting only the best stuff. The process of doing research increases your knowledge. And this is a real confidence-builder to the speaker. The best speakers in my experience are also active practitioners in the fields they speak about. Their expertise stems from a combination of research and real-world experience. As Cicero once said, "No man can be eloquent in a subject he does not understand."

Organize Your Material

The best way to organize your thoughts is to make notes on index cards. Jot down one idea or one piece of information per card. You may also want to make a rough outline of your talk, and then arrange the cards according to the topics on the outline. This helps you arrange the material in logical sequence, and also reveals which areas require further research. Choose a sequence that fits the materials; see Chapter 3 for ideas and suggestions.

Every talk has three parts: beginning, middle, and end. In the beginning, you state your purpose and provide a preview of what will be covered. This preview is a quick summary of the outline of your talk. In the middle, you go through the outline point by point. Be sure to cover every topic promised in the preview. In the end, you sum up your talk and ask for any appropriate action (for example, a scientist might ask top management for funds to pursue a particular avenue of research or a salesperson might ask a group of prospects for an order).

Interact With your Audience

While talking, make eye contact with individuals in the audience. Look at a person and act as if you're speaking directly to him or her. After a minute, pick someone else. Doing so helps you communicate with the audience rather than just read to them. Speak loudly enough that people in the back can hear you. If people are too far away, ask them to move closer before you start. Use gestures, tone, and volume to emphasize key points. Stick to your main points as outlined in the visuals and your notes. Don't wander off on tangents.

If you intend to distribute a leave-behind (such as a bound booklet containing copies of the visuals or a reprint of the speech), say so before you begin your talk. That way, the audience knows they don't have to take notes and they can sit back, relax, and enjoy the speech. But don't hand out the leave-behind until after the presentation. If you distribute it before or during the talk, people will read it and ignore the speaker: you. Leave time for a question-and-answer period. Take all questions after the talk, rather than allowing interruptions. At the conclusion, summarize your main points and tell the audience what action they should take, or at least what you expect them to have learned, or want them to believe.

Use Visuals

Too many PowerPoint presentations are either nothing more than bullet points on word slides or graphics lifted from available resources (white papers, websites, brochures) and pasted into a slide with no rhyme or reason. When you are creating your PowerPoint slides, poster boards, flip charts, or whatever type of visual aide you prefer, understand the basic types of visuals and how they can be used to illustrate your subject, as shown on page 142.

Visual aids have become standard in business and technical presentations, and with good reason. Visuals reinforce the presentation and help the audience remember your talk after it's over. Visuals also serve to focus audience attention on the speaker. According to a study by the Wharton School, the use of visuals results in a greater percentage of the audience agreeing with the speaker's point of view. When visuals are used, participants come to a decision faster. And they perceive the speaker as more professional, more credible, more interesting, and better prepared than speakers who don't use visuals.

With today's modern computer graphics, visuals are affordable to firms of every size. Media types include PowerPoint and 35mm slides, overhead transparencies, and flip charts. When preparing your visuals, select the medium that will convey your message most effectively. A seminar on how to improve your golf swing might combine video of Tiger Woods with a live demonstration by the instructor. A professor giving a talk on how to enjoy classical music would of course play short selections from classical CDs and perhaps also have a piano in the room to demonstrate certain musical principles.

The key to creating successful visuals is not to cram too much onto a single slide. Each slide should contain no more than one simple graph or chart, or five short lines of text. A good test of legibility for 35mm color slides is to hold the slide at arm's length and read it. If you can't make out the words,

Visuals and Their Application

Type of Visual	This Visual Shows
Photograph or drawing	What something looks like
Map	Where it is located
Diagram	How it works or is organized
Schematic	How it is assembled or put together
Graph	How much one variables changes as another variable is changing
Pie chart	Proportions and percentages
Bar chart	Comparison among quantities
Table	A body of data
Flow chart	Steps in a process

chances are the people in the back of the room won't be able to read the slide when it is projected. For PowerPoint, print the slide full size on an 8½ by 11-inch sheet of paper and hold it at arm's length. If you have to squint to read the captions, labels, and bullets, cut verbiage and make the text larger.

> "Use visual aids to help make your point. If your audience will understand your point without PowerPoint, don't use PowerPoint."
> – Alan Sharpe

Arrive early to check out the room and the equipment. Anyone who doesn't think this is important hasn't heard the words, "But no one said you wanted a projector!" If possible, run through the talk in the conference room before the audience arrives. Check the temperature and adjust the thermostat as needed. Make sure the seating arrangement is the way you want it. Find the light controls and set the lighting to your liking. Do a sound-check using the microphone. If you are being recorded, the technician will want to check that, too. Hook up your laptop to the LCD projector and run through all your slides. Turn on the projector when you first get to the room. "If the bulb in a projector is going to fail, it will usually do so when the projector is first turned on," says Terry Smith. "So turn it on a little early and leave it on. And ask for a spare bulb."

Before you speak, head to the bathroom or your hotel room for an appearance check. Make sure your clothes are all tucked in, with no embarrassing gaps or zippers left open. (I had a math professor in college who wore leisure suits so faded they looked mildewed, and he never remembered to close his fly.) Men should tighten the knot in their tie. Comb or brush your hair. I recommend people who travel and speak frequently get their hair cut short, because it is easier to keep in place, especially on windy days. Brush your teeth and use a mouthwash; you don't want bad breath to ruin the audience's impression of you when they chat with you up close during breaks or after your talk. And make a conscious effort to smile at least part of the time.

Don't Put Your Audience into a PowerPoint Coma

I use PowerPoint in all my talks. Most speakers do. It is today's accepted standard for presentation visuals. Yet as useful a tool as it is, PowerPoint, when misused, can actually make a presentation more boring. PowerPoint has become the de facto standard for making presentations in the corporate world today. Yet nearly everyone (even Dilbert) talks about how boring PowerPoint presentations can be. Why is that?

To begin with, relying on PowerPoint risks taking the focus away from where it should be—the content, message, and audience—and puts it on the technology.

Second, it encourages a conformity that robs speakers and presentations of their individuality. All PowerPoint presentations tend to look alike after awhile.

Third, it is a becoming an overused medium that people are now beginning to equate with boring presentations. Many bad presentations have been prepared with PowerPoint. I believe the very use of the medium itself can be a signal to some audience members that says, "Prepared to be bored."

Fourth, it renders many speakers ineffective, or at least less effective. When the speaker is focusing on her clicker, keyboard, or computer screen, she is not focusing on—or interacting with—her audience, a key requisite for a successful talk.

Fifth, it locks the speaker into the prepared slides, reducing spontaneity, adlibbing, and the valuable ability to adjust the presentation in response to audience reaction and interest—another requisite for a successful talk.

Finally, it can literally put the audience to sleep. What's the first step in preparing an audience to view a PowerPoint presentation? Dimming the lights—an action proven to induce drowsiness.

Can you really give an effective presentation without building it around PowerPoint? Of course. But let's say you are putting together a presentation for an event that requires speakers to use PowerPoint. What can you do to make it more effective? Here are four suggestions:

1. Don't have the projector on all the time. Use PowerPoint selectively, not throughout the entire presentation. When there's a valuable picture to show, show it. When you're through with it, project a title slide, or turn off the projector and turn the lights back on. The brightness rouses the audience out of their darkness-induced stupor. In a darkened room, it's too easy to close your eyes and nod off a bit.

2. Use visuals only when they communicate more effectively than words. If you are talking about quality, having the word "Quality" on the screen adds little to your point. On the other hand, if you want to explain what an aardvark looks like, there are no words that can do it as effectively as simply showing a picture.

3. Consider adding other media as supplements or even alternatives to PowerPoint. When I taught telephone selling, the sound of a ringing telephone and a prop (a toy telephone) engaged the trainees in a way computer slides could not.

4. Design your presentation so that, if there is a problem with the computer equipment, you can go on without it. There's nothing more embarrassing than to see a speaker fall apart because he can't find the right slide. Use visuals as an enhancement, not a crutch. Always carry a hard copy of your PowerePoint with you just in case.

Voice: Pace, Tone, Volume, and Projection

Speak in a natural manner, much like you would when having a conversation with a friend. Most venues have microphones, and most speakers should take advantage of them. Even if you have the kind of resonant, booming voice that can project throughout a conference room and be heard without a microphone, use of the microphone can save your voice. Unless you are an experienced speaker or teacher, you will be shocked how quickly your voice tires and you get hoarse when giving a longer talk. The microphone can extend the time period during which you can speak comfortably and without undue strain.

Although you can vary speaking speed, keep it even for the most part; rapid enough so people are not bored, but not so fast that you become difficult to understand. The main voice tool to use for effect is not speed but volume. Softening your voice can convey emotion and create a more serious or somber mood. Speaking more loudly can help make an important point more powerfully and stir a crowd; listen to the "I Have a Dream" speech of Dr. Martin Luther King to hear this principle in action. Pauses are also an effective speaker's tool. In particular, a pause can help focus the audience's attention on you, even create suspense and dramatic effect.

Props and Gimmicks

I am a big believer in using props, both visual and auditory, if you desire to do so and are comfortable with them. Props add dimensionality to a talk. Instead of just looking at the speaker or a screen, the audience's interest is piqued when you hold a potato and a straw, or three rubber balls, or a pair of socks in front of them. They become instantly curious. Why is the speaker holding these things? What have they got to do with the subject matter? What is he going to do with them? Will he put on the socks? Juggle the balls?

Ideally, the props should tie in with an idea or point you are presenting. One speaker, teaching problem solving skills, hands out a raw potato and paper straw to everyone in the audience. He asks them to put the straw through the potato without using a knife, pen, or any other tool. As it turns out, you can drive even a flimsy paper straw through a hard, raw potato if you plunge it into the potato in one rapid straight-on motion, much the same way a hurricane can drive a wooden plank through a brick wall. My friend Richard Armstrong has a talk on advertising in which he makes the point that the message of the ad must resonate with the reader. He illustrates the concept

The Keeper of the Time

Here is a fun way to keep track of the time without checking your watch.

At the beginning say, "Since I don't have a good sense of time, I need one person in the group to be Keeper of the Time. This involves shouting out the word time in a loud and obnoxious manner every X minutes." In an hour session, X can be every 15 minutes; in a full day session, X can be every 60 minutes or every 30 minutes.

If no one volunteers, I hold up a copy of my book and say I will give it free to the audience member who will be Keeper of the Time; several people immediately raise their hands. "But you have to be on time, loud, and obnoxious," I say to the person so everyone can hear. "I can judge whether you are on time and loud; but the class will judge whether you are obnoxious enough. Every time you fail to be on time, loud, or obnoxious, I will rip some pages out of the book, decreasing its value." This gets a laugh—and no, I never actually rip the book.

by showing how one tuning fork, when struck and placed next to another tuning fork, will cause the second fork to resonate at the same frequency as the first, even though they are not touching.

Not every prop or gimmick ties directly into your message or illustrates a point; though with thought, you can often find a way to relate the trick or device to your message. In a sports psychology class he teaches, motivational speaker Rob Gilbert starts by holding a $100 bill in his hand and stretching it out to the audience. He then stays silent. After a minute of uncomfortable silence, one attendee invariably gets up, hesitantly makes his way to the front of the room, and gingerly takes the money from Rob, who allows him to do so without resistance. And the attendee keeps the money. In one class, a student asks, "Why did you do this?" Rob answered, "Twenty years from now, you'll remember this class because of it."

Overcoming Poor Speaking Habits

Many people who can otherwise deliver a useful talk have their performance marred by a bad speech habit. For years, while an otherwise competent and well-received speaker, I frequently said "you know" during my talks. Having an attendee or your boss point this out to you won't cure it, because you just don't believe it. And that's because you don't hear or notice it when you speak. If you did, you wouldn't do it. The quickest cure is to audiotape or videotape your presentation, and then listen to or watch it. You will be absolutely horrified—mortified—to hear the embarrassing speaking flaw. When you do, your brain will set up a mental alert system, similar to warning message on a PC. From then on, when you commit the error in speaking, you'll instantly notice it. And after noticing it, your brain will be on "red alert" to make sure it doesn't happen. More than likely, the poor speaking habit will either decrease in frequency to the point where no listener is aware of it, or disappear altogether.

Body Language and Eye Contact

In Chapter 1, we discussed how the key to being a good speaker is to not "give a speech" and instead to just "have a conversation." A good conversationalist makes eye contact with the other person, while an awkward conversationalist avoids eye contact. So as outlined in Chapter 1, talk to the people in your audience by making eye contact with them one at a time. You don't have to maintain eye contact with the audience at all times, but make sure you do it with different audience members throughout your talk. When I speak, I look primarily in three directions: at the audience, my speaker notes, and the PowerPoint slides on the screen.

You may need to look at your watch occasionally to make sure you are on track. At some meetings, a staff member is assigned the task of keeping the speaker on time by holding up signs indicating the number of minutes remaining: 15, 10, 5, and 1. Or they may flash these numbers with the fingers on their hands. You may feel the need to get a reading on time remaining earlier, which looking at a wall clock or your watch can tell you. But don't be too obvious about it. When the audience sees you glancing at your watch every other minute, they interpret that to mean you want the session to be over.

Posture and Position

Some speakers remain fixed behind the podium, and some step out from behind the podium and walk around on the stage. I recommend stepping off the stage and walking around the room. Do not practice dramatic gestures or deliberate postures or poses; just stand, walk, and move as you do in everyday life. A speaker's coach once criticized me for putting my hands in my pockets during one of my talks. I wouldn't leave them there the whole time, but I think varying your motions and movements breaks up the monotony of a lecture.

I am a person who likes to clown, and I let that natural impulse take over when I speak. If I am in a classroom with a chalkboard that needs to be erased, I say, "Remember how your teacher in school told you to clean the eraser?" I then bang them together to create a cloud of chalk dust and cough in an exaggerated fashion; it always gets a laugh. My rule of thumb is that if an idea occurs to you spontaneously during a presentation, do it unless it has the potential to be offensive to someone in the audience.

For instance, during one talk, I got stuck on a word I could not get out of my mouth clearly. After flubbing it several times, I quickly reached out, took a small glass of water from the table next to me, and threw it into my face. The class was stunned for half a second, and then broke out into laughter. I dried my hair and face with a cloth napkin from the table and continued speaking with interruption, as if nothing had happened.

In another class where I taught direct mail to the marketing department of a software company, most of the attendees were very young. At one point, a reference to Eminem came up, and a woman in the front row made a tentative start at singing the chorus of one of his rap songs. I instantly joined her, and we started moving our hands to the beat, and then everyone joined us. They absolutely loved it, and they were my fast friends from that point on. I realize this may not be your style, so just do what works for you.

Of course, none of this may be your style at all. And that's the point: Be your most natural self. Audiences can sense a speaker who is genuine and sincere. They want you to be a real person, not a stage act or a stiff. The less you put on an act, and the more you act and talk like your everyday self, the better.

Microphones and Audiovisual Aids

For most speaking engagements, the speaker is asked in advance to specify what equipment is needed for the room. If you use PowerPoint, you are expected to bring it loaded on your own laptop. You then need an LCD projector with connection cable and a screen. The microphone can be on a stand at the podium, a wireless hand-held, or a lavaliere, which is a portable clipped to your necktie, shirt, or blouse. I prefer a wireless hand-held or lavaliere, because they allow me to walk around the room unencumbered by a cord. You should stand where you are comfortable, but if you can be comfortable walking around instead of staying on stage, I urge you to do it. Stepping down from the podium and out into the crowd among the attendees makes you seem more a part of the crowd and less superior and stand offish.

If there is a wired hand-held microphone on a stand at the podium, I check to make sure the cord is long enough so I can at least walk as far as the second or third row of seats. Often the cords are taped to the floor or podium to prevent you from tripping on them, so I pull up the tape and toss it away before my talk starts, giving me the mobility I prefer. Your mobility may be limited if the meeting is being videotaped, in which case the videographer will tell you where you can and can't stand. Also be careful about stepping in front of the LCD projector and blocking the screen. I occasionally do this by

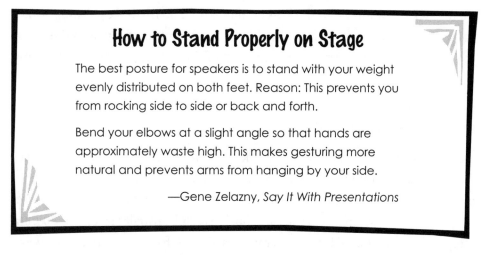

How to Stand Properly on Stage

The best posture for speakers is to stand with your weight evenly distributed on both feet. Reason: This prevents you from rocking side to side or back and forth.

Bend your elbows at a slight angle so that hands are approximately waste high. This makes gesturing more natural and prevents arms from hanging by your side.

—Gene Zelazny, *Say It With Presentations*

accident. If I become aware that I am blocking the screen, I step out of the light beam, but keep my hands in, and make a quick shadow puppet. Again, it always gets a laugh.

Preventing Technical Mishaps From Ruining Your Talk

The problem with the growing popularity of PowerPoint is that speakers become wholly dependent on it, just as in the 20th century, they were similarly dependent on their 35 mm color slides. When the audiovisual project device malfunctions, they become flustered; many cannot deliver the presentation without it.

When I worked for Terry Smith in the late 1970s at Westinghouse, he told me, "When you give a presentation, never allow yourself to become separated from your slides." Today, this means keep your PowerPoint on your laptop and always carry it with you. Further, carry a hard copy printout of your slides to every talk you give. Design your presentation in such a way that, should the projector fail or your laptop crash, you can still give your talk or a modified version of it that stands independent of the visual. I like to have triple back-ups for my talks: In addition to the PowerPoint stored on my laptop, I carry a hard copy printout with me. I also e-mail the PowerPoint in advance to the meeting planner. Lastly, I carry a back-up copy of the PowerPoint on a CD in my laptop bag.

Length and Timing

Talks can vary from a ten-minute workplace presentation to a two-day intensive seminar. How long should yours be? The event and meeting planner often dictate length. Luncheon and after dinner talks to local groups and local chapters of professional societies and business clubs usually last 20 to 30 minutes, with an additional five to ten minutes allotted for questions and answers.

For technical sessions at major conferences and national expositions, speakers generally get 45 to 75 minutes. For a one-hour talk, prepare a 45-

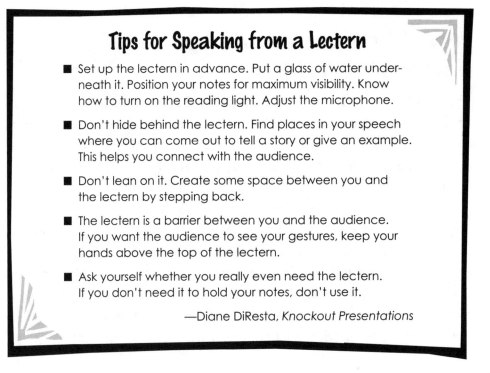

Tips for Speaking from a Lectern

- Set up the lectern in advance. Put a glass of water underneath it. Position your notes for maximum visibility. Know how to turn on the reading light. Adjust the microphone.

- Don't hide behind the lectern. Find places in your speech where you can come out to tell a story or give an example. This helps you connect with the audience.

- Don't lean on it. Create some space between you and the lectern by stepping back.

- The lectern is a barrier between you and the audience. If you want the audience to see your gestures, keep your hands above the top of the lectern.

- Ask yourself whether you really even need the lectern. If you don't need it to hold your notes, don't use it.

—Diane DiResta, *Knockout Presentations*

minute talk. You'll probably start five minutes late to allow for late arrivals, and the last ten minutes can be a more informal question and answer session.

The luckiest speakers are those who get invited to participate in panels. If you are on a panel consisting of three or four experts plus a moderator, it's likely that you'll simply be asked to respond to questions from the moderator or the audience, eliminating the need to prepare a talk. Or, each panelist might give a short lecture, usually just 15 minutes.

Richard Armstrong, a freelance corporate speechwriter, says most of the speeches he writes are 20 minutes in length. James Welch, author of *The Speech Writing Guide* (John Wiley & Sons), says that a typed double-spaced page of manuscript should take the speaker two and one-half minutes to deliver. This means an eight-page double-spaced manuscript, which is about 2,000 words, will take 20 minutes to deliver as a speech.

That's about 100 words a minute. Some speakers are faster, talking at 120 to 150 words a minute or more. So the 20-minute talk can really be anywhere from eight to ten typed pages.

The most important thing is to not exceed the allotted time. If you are given 20 minutes with an additional ten minutes for questions and answers, stop after 20 minutes. People won't mind if you finish a bit early, but they will become fidgety and start looking at their watches if your time limit is up and you don't seem even near finished.

Since most of us cannot concentrate on two things at once, such as giving a talk and watching a clock, I always ask someone in the audience to be the timekeeper to keep me on track. For example, if giving a 45-minute talk, I ask him to shout out "TIME!" every 15 minutes. The first two interruptions tell me where I am and how closely I'm on track; the last tells me to stop and shut up.

As a rule, shorter is usually better than longer. "Have you ever wished a presentation were longer or more complicated?" asks former advertising executive Michael Gates Gill in his book *How Starbucks Saved My Life*. "The best presentations are simple and short."

Closings That Get You a Standing Ovation

Here's a simple trick, taught to me by motivational speaker Rob Gilbert, that can help get you a standing ovation or close to it. After making your final comments, look out over the audience and say, "Thanks for your attention." Pause for one second, and then say with great sincerity, "You've been a great group." For some reason, this close communicates to the attendees that you really appreciate them. They feel compelled to show that they really appreciate you. Immediately after you say "You've been a great group," they will burst into applause. If you gave a solid presentation, and you stand there as they applaud and smile humbly, you may find some of the attendees rising to their feet. Others follow, and you have your standing ovation. Enjoy it—You've earned it!

Is a standing ovation the most important yardstick by which you are judged by a speaker? No. Evaluations are more important. So is feedback from attendees weeks or months after the session that says they put your ideas into action and they worked. But it doesn't hurt to have them clapping and standing at the end, and sure beats catcalls, anemic applause, or silence.

Tips for Speakers

Dr. Rob Gilbert offers these 42 tips for giving great talks.

1. Write your own introduction and mail it to the sponsoring organization in advance of your appearance.

2. Establish rapport with the audience early.

3. What you say is not as important as how you say it.

4. Self-effacing humor works best.

5. Ask the audience questions.

6. Don't give a talk—have a conversation.

7. In an average audience, 30 percent of the people will never ask the speaker a question.

8. A little bit of nervous tension is probably good for you.

9. Extremely nervous? Use rapport building, not stress reduction, techniques.

10. The presentation does not have to be great to be useful to your attendees. Tell your audience that if they get one good idea out of your talk, it will have been worthwhile for them.

11. People want stories, not information.

12. Get the audience involved.

13. People pay more for entertainment than education. (Proof: The average college professor would have to work ten centuries to earn what Oprah Winfrey makes in a year.)

14. You have to love what you are doing. (Dr. Gilbert has 8,000 cassette tapes of speeches and listens to these tapes three to four hours a day.)

15. The first time you give a particular talk, it will not be great.

16. The three hardest audiences to address: engineers, accountants, and high school students.

17. If heckled, you can turn any situation around ("verbal aikido").

18. Communicate from the Heart + Have an Important Message = Speaking Success.

19. You can't please everybody, so don't even try. Some will like you and your presentation and some won't.

20. Ask your audience how you are doing and what they need to hear from you to rate you higher.

21. Be flexible and spontaneous. Play off your audience.

22. Be totally authentic.

23. To announce a break say, "We'll take a five-minute break now, so I'll expect you back here in 10 minutes." It always gets a laugh.

24. To get them back in the room (if you are the speaker), go out into the hall and shout, "He's starting; he's starting!"

25. Courage is to feel the fear and do it anyway. The only way to overcome what you fear is to do it.

26. If panic strikes, just give the talk and keep your mouth moving. The fear will subside in a minute or two.

27. In speaking, writing, teaching, and marketing, everything you see, read, hear, do, or experience is grist for the mill.

28. Tell touching stories.

29. If the stories are about you, be the goat, not the hero. People like speakers who are humble; audiences hate bragging and braggarts.

30. Join Toastmasters. Take a Dale Carnegie course in public speaking. Join the National Speakers Association.

31. Go hear the great speakers and learn from them.

32. If you borrow stories or techniques from other speakers, adapt this material and use it in your own unique way.

33. Use audiovisual aids if you wish, but not as a crutch.

34. When presenting a daylong workshop, make the afternoon shorter than the morning.

35. Asking people to perform a simple physical exercise (stretching, Simon Says, etc.) as an activity during a break can increase their energy level and overcome lethargy.

36. People love storytellers.

37. Today's most popular speaking topic: Change (in business, society, lifestyles, etc.) and how to cope with it.

38. There is no failure—just feedback.

39. At the conclusion of your talk, tell your audience that they were a great audience even if they were not.

40. Ask for applause using this closing: "You've been a wonderful audience. [pause]. Thank you very much."

41. If you want to become a good speaker give as many talks as you can to as many groups as you can, even if you don't get paid at first. You will improve as you gain experience. (Dr. Gilbert has some speeches he has given more than 1,000 times.)

42. Cruise lines frequently offer speakers free trips in exchange for a brief lecture during the cruise. And they do not demand top, experienced speakers.

Successful presentations can get results!

CHAPTER 9

Audience Management

The two most important people in speaking are the speaker and the listener and of those, the listener is by far the more important.

The mediocre speaker reads a talk without awareness of or connection with the audience. The competent speaker is as aware of the audience, and their reaction to his talk, as he is of his notes or slides. Great speakers tailor content, pace, and delivery "on the fly" to ensure a superior learning experience for the audience. But whatever level you are at, your focus is always on pleasing the audience; giving them what they want, teaching them what they need to know about your topic, and making sure they enjoy the experience. In this chapter, we'll look at how to understand the audience's expectations and deliver a presentation that meets or exceeds it.

Client Needs Assessment

When speaking, you have two parties you have to please: the people who attend the meeting and the people who arranged the meeting. In most instances, the attendees are the people who are there to absorb your content. But the meeting planner is your client. Often, their objectives are overlapping, but not identical.

How do you determine what the client wants? We've already covered that in detail in Chapter 2. The best tool for assessing the meeting planner's needs is my Pre-Program Questionnaire, reprinted in Appendix II. Just give a copy to the meeting planner. Ask him to fill it out and return it to you far in advance of the seminar date. The completed questionnaire tells you who is in the audience, what the meeting planner wants you to talk to them about, how much they already know about it, what they need to know, and the problems they face that the knowledge you impart should help them overcome.

Attendee Pre-event Audits

I always determine the clients' needs by requiring them to fill out and return my Pre-Program Questionnaire and by talking with them on the phone prior to the speaking engagement. Doing so enables me to tailor my talk to their objectives and goals.

I also like to do the same with the audience. Remember, there are two parties you as a speaker must please. The meeting planner is one; the audience is the other. It's possible to please your attendees even if the meeting planner isn't 100 percent satisfied. But if the audience is not happy, they will complain to the meeting planner, and he or she will not be happy no matter how much your program complies with the original instructions.

There are several ways you can assess the audience's needs to ensure delivery of a talk that makes them happy. The most effective is with an Audience Audit Form. This is a questionnaire that the attendees, not the meeting plan-

Which Matters Most: Technique or Content?

"The information you deliver and its relevance to your audience is far more important than your platform technique or presentation skills. Content is audience-centered; platform skills are speaker-centered. The only function of the latter is to enhance the former."

—Alan Weiss, *Money Talks*

ner, fill out and returns to you (usually through the meeting planner, not directly) prior to the event. I use different audit forms tailored to each of the topics I speak on. In Appendix IV, I reprint the Audience Audit Form I use for my writing seminars.

I always use Audience Audit Forms when doing corporate training. We know who will be attending, and the meeting planner can require employees to complete and return the form. When speaking to large groups as conventions and association meetings, you don't know which of the attendees will go to your session, so using an audit form is not always possible.

One alternative is to ask the meeting planner if there are members of the association that are definitely attending. If so, ask permission to call and briefly interview a couple of the members. These interviews can quickly bring you up to speed on industry issues, problems, and what the audience wants to learn. If the meeting planner cannot arrange these phone interviews prior to the speech, there is another alternative: the pre-seminar walk-around.

Pre-Seminar Walk Around

As the speaker, you will arrive in the seminar room 30 to 60 minutes prior to the start of your program to familiarize yourself with your surroundings, check audiovisuals, and otherwise get ready. Some attendees will begin to trickle in as the hour approaches. If you are speaking to a group of 20 to 50 people, it is not unusual to have half a dozen or more attendees in the room 10 or even 15 minutes before the start time.

Most speakers I observe do not talk to these early arrivers other than to speak the word "hello." They are wasting an important opportunity. I step out from behind the podium, walk out into the audience, and introduce myself and chat individually with my early arrivers for a minute or two each. I ask them their name, company, position, and this question: "If you could get one thing out of this session, what would it be?" After my walk-around, I have gained two key pieces of information that can help me deliver a better talk.

First, I know the names of at least half a dozen attendees who, to the other people who come in on time or late, it may seem I already know somehow. When appropriate, I may, during my talk, refer to them by name, asking them a question or soliciting an opinion. Also, I make sure that I address at least some of the points they give me in the answer to their question, "If you could get one thing out of this session, what would it be?"

With groups of 20 trainees or fewer in a full-day training class, we go around the room. I ask everyone their name, their position and job function,

Taking Questions from the Audience

"It is a good idea to tell your listeners before you begin that you will open the meeting to questions from the audience at the conclusion of your talk. Your listeners will look forward to taking an active part in the talk and enjoy asking specific questions about your points. A relaxed question-and-answer period will probably results in lots of fun and enlightenment, for you as well."

—Vernon Howard, *Talking to an Audience*

why they are in the class, and the most important thing they would hope to learn. I take notes on flip charts of the topics they want covered, tape the flip charts to the wall, and check off the items as we cover each. That way, at the end of the day, I have covered what they wanted to know, and they can see that I have done so.

Customization and Personalization

A standard speech or program is a canned speech or lecture. The speaker delivers essentially the same talk, regardless of venue or audience.

A customized speech is your standard speech moderately altered to fit the group or organization that invited you to give the talk. The degree of alteration depends on the client, the speaker, and how much the situation demands it. When speaking at a convention of printers, the degree of customization can be as little as substituting the word "printers" for "small business owners" in your standard talk. Or it can be as extensive as researching and incorporating case studies, ideas, and strategies specifically for printers into the seminar.

A personalized speech is a customized speech where the case studies, examples, and data are drawn from a corporate sponsor's specific business. In addition, the training materials are imprinted with the corporate sponsor's logo and may even be customized further; e.g., a lesson teaching a business procedure may be made specific to the equipment they use or sell.

A licensed speech is a presentation that you prepare and own, then license to a company or association for their speakers and trainers to present. You give the licensee your speaker notes and scripts, PowerPoint, questionnaires, audit forms, and any other materials necessary to deliver the talk. You are paid a fee each time the presentation is given.

When I began giving talks in the early 1980s, an overwhelming number of speakers delivered canned talks, and audiences expected and accepted it. Today, audiences have shorter attention spans, and can easily get general information from a Google search. What they expect and demand from live presentations today is great content from an expert, customized to their interests and needs.

Preparing and Distributing Handouts

Must you have a leave-behind? For a keynote to a large audience at a conference or meeting, a handout could be considered optional, although I would opt for having one. In virtually every other speaking situation, a handout is highly recommended if not absolutely mandatory (at some conferences, the sponsor actually requires speakers to use PowerPoint and supply their slides to be printed as a hand-out).

The leave-behind can take one of several formats. It can be hard copy of the PowerPoint slides, brochures, article reprints, or reprints of the narration (with visuals incorporated, if possible). It can be the full text of your talk, an outline, just the visuals, or a report or article on a topic that is either related to the presentation topic or that expands on one of the subtopics you touched on briefly in the talk. If you use PowerPoint, you can just print out your PowerPoint presentation and use that as the handout.

Every handout should contain your company name, address, phone, and fax, and if possible a full resource box with a brief summary of who you are and what you do, as should *every* marketing document you produce.

If the handout is the full text of your talk or a set of fairly comprehensive notes, tell the audience before starting, "There's no need to take notes. We have hard copies of this presentation for you to take home." This relieves listeners of the burden of note taking, freeing them to concentrate on your talk.

Handouts such as transcripts of a speech, articles, reports, or other materials with lots of copy should be handed out *after* the talk, not before. If you hand them out before you step up to the podium, the audience will read the printed materials and ignore you. You can hand out reproductions of visuals or pages with just a few bullet points in advance, so attendees can write notes directly on them.

Why do you need handouts? They enhance learning. But the main reason to give handouts is to ensure that every attendee (most of whom are potential customers, or you wouldn't be addressing the group) walks away with a piece of paper containing information on what you offer and how to contact you. That way, when the person goes to work the next morning and thinks, "That was an interesting talk; maybe I should contact them to talk about how they can help us," he or she has your phone number in hand. Without it, response to your talk will be zero or near zero; most people are too busy, lazy, or indifferent to start tracking you down if they don't

Make sure your name, company name, job title, and at least one way to contact you – phone number, website URL, e-mail address, postal address – are printed on all your handouts.

have immediate access to your contact information. Another reason is to further ensure attendee satisfaction. Even with a great seminar, attendees feel they get more value when they walk away with some hard copy reference materials they can share with their team when they get back to work.

It's important to give a useful, interesting, information-packed talk that convinces prospects you know what you are talking about and makes them want to talk with you about doing work for them. But without the contact information immediately in hand, the prospect's interest and curiosity quickly evaporates. Since you cannot tell in advance who in the audience will want to follow up with you and who will not, your goal is to get everybody or as many people as possible to pick up and take home your handout material.

There are several ways to distribute handouts at your talk. The most common is to leave the materials on a table, either in the back of the room or at the registration table where people sign in for the meeting or your session.

But this is not effective. Most people will walk right by the table without picking up the material. Many won't even notice the table or stack of handouts. Even if you point out the table and say that reprints are available, many won't take one. And you might feel embarrassed at the silence that follows your announcement; it makes you seem less authoritative, more of a promoter.

Another technique is to put a copy of your handout on each seat in the room about a half hour before the start of your presentation. Most people will pick it up, look at it; about one-quarter to one-half will take it with them when they leave, and half or more will leave it on the chair. Disadvantages? People may read the handout and not pay attention to your presentation. Also, some people resent this approach, seeing it as being too pushy and too salesy, especially if your handout material includes an order form for your products or a brochure about your company and your services.

Handling Hecklers and Other Disruptive Influences

It happens: You are talking, and you hear noise emanating from the audience. You look for the source of disruption, and see a couple of attendees having a private conversation at a decibel level that interferes with your presentation. In business presentations, hecklers are much rarer. Stand-up comics and humorous speakers are the most likely to get heckled; humor is subjective, and some people resent speakers who try to be funny, especially when they feel they are not.

Handling disruptions is not as straightforward as you think. In an ideal world, you would be able to demand that they get up and leave. Teachers do this, sending kids who misbehave out of the classroom and down to the principal's office. But you are not a principal, and your attendees are not kids. They are adults whose seats have been paid for. So you have to handle them with in a manner that is firm but polite, and not angry, abusive, or insulting.

There are a number of techniques that can work. Once, already discussed, is speaker silence. Stop talking, stand at the front of the stage in an at ease position, look at the offenders, and do nothing. The room will turn quiet and

Handling Hecklers

Often there is one person in the audience who is cranky, difficult, and vocal. To get him on your side, wait until he says something that you agree with to some degree. Praise his observation, state your agreement, and compliment him on being so astute. This can help diffuse his hostility and get him on your side.

others will turn to look at them. The troublemakers will realize they are the center of negative attention, and they will quiet down so you can resume your talk. Another simple yet effective method is to step down from the platform and walk over to the offending party while you simply continue to talk. When they see you are standing next to them, they will quiet down in a hurry. It also works to address them from the platform by saying, "Guys, is there something you want to share with the group?" They will look down or away, mumble "no, nothing," and knock off the noise and nuisance.

Other do's and don'ts for handling hecklers and others who interrupt:

- DON'T get angry or emotional with the heckler. He wants to upset you. If you get angry, he wins.

- DO pull the person aside during the break. Tell him how his actions are disrupting the seminar for the other attendees. If you have the authority to do so, give him the option of not staying, and offer a full refund if he has paid.

- DON'T argue or debate directly with the person. See the section on page 169 on handling audience members who challenge what you are saying.

- DO stay cool and calm when heckled. You may be flustered. You may be upset. You may be ticked off. But don't show it. Act nonchalant, as if the interruption is no big deal to you.

■ DO ask the meeting planner to intervene if the disruption continues. You are there to deliver a lecture at their request, and the interruption makes the meeting planner look bad, not just you.

Audience Question and Answer

You can take questions from the audience at the end of your talk, at various intervals during your talk, or whenever someone raises their hand to ask a question. Just make clear to your audience your preference. If you take only questions at the end, tell them to jot down any questions that come to mind during your talk, and then ask during the Q&A period following the presentation.

A lively Q&A adds energy and interest to any seminar. So it's to your advantage to have the audience ask questions. Some groups are not shy about asking questions and will bombard you. When you are asked a question by an audience member, repeat is loudly and clearly so everyone can hear the question. Then give your answer.

Amplify the Audience

"If the audience is allowed to ask questions or make comments, you run the risk of having a long-winded attendee hijack your microphone as he rambles on."

"Solution: Have specially designated *microphone runners* who are responsible for moving to the person in the audience who wishes to talk. The microphone runner physically keeps a hold of the microphone as the attendee is speaking. If the runner relinquishes the microphone to the attendee, you have a far greater chance of losing control of things."

—Bret Ridgeway, *View from the Back*

Many speakers give one of the attendees or the meeting planner a couple of "seed" questions; questions prepared in advance by the speaker. If no one has a question when the speaker asks for them, the attendee or meeting planner jumps in by asking one of the seed questions—of course not identifying it as such. Invariably, this makes the other attendees less shy, and you will get several other questions. Another technique for getting the Q&A started is for the speaker to offer a copy of one of his books or some other small gift to the person who asks the first question.

What if you get asked a question to which you don't know the answer? One easy way out is to open it to the group, saying, "That's a great question, Fred. Folks, what do you think"? Then you just sit back and moderate the debate. Or, if no one in the room knows, you or one of the attendees can volunteer to research the question and get back to everyone with an answer.

Facing a Challenge

What happens when an attendee challenges something you say or your authority to say it? The best approach is to not engage in an argument with any audience members or express annoyance or behave in an adversarial manner. Instead, acknowledge what they are saying without agreeing or disagreeing with it. One way is to defer discussion until after your talk by saying, "That's an interesting point and one I can't fully answer here. Why don't we talk about it after the workshop?" This essentially puts an end to the matter. What rational person could say no to such a reasonable request? If you have to catch a plane immediately after your talk, offer to continue the discussion via e-mail when both of you return to your offices.

An alternative tactic is to let your audience argue on your behalf, especially if you sense they are in agreement with your point of view and not the interrupter's. You can say, "Guys, what are your thoughts on what Dave just said?" When all else fails, a polite way of ending a debate is simply to say, "I understand what you are saying; for now, let's just agree to disagree."

A third tactic, applicable in disputes for subjects that are largely a matter of opinion, is to acknowledge that you are giving your opinion, that it is only an opinion, and that the attendee's opinion may also be valid. On the other hand, if you are sure you are right, you can choose to back your opinion with whatever proof you have available. But don't be obnoxious or arrogant when you do so.

For example, when teaching business writing to a group of engineers at a manufacturing company, I advocated writing in a simple, natural style. One of the older attendees insisted I was wrong; he had been taught that writing should be formal. I pointed out that it was when he was starting out, but that styles change, and modern business writing is more conversational and less formal. He would not accept it. I said in a polite tone, not at all hostile, "You may be right. But I have taught writing to thousands of students, reviewed or written thousands of business documents over the last 20 years, and written over 70 published books. So I can only give you my opinion based on my own observations and experience. Yours may be different, but I know what works for my other students and what their employers look for in their writing."

Hostile Audiences

Hostile audiences come in several varieties. The mildest form of audience hostility is indifference; lack of interest in your topic, and no desire to be in the seminar. Corporate employees who are sent by their supervisors to training seminars they don't want to attend can fall into this category. They are not hostile in the sense of being angry with you, the speaker, though they may resent being forced to listen to you. A good example is the engineers I talked about earlier in the book who are sent to my technical writing seminars. In Chapter 2, I gave you a strategy for coping with this mild hostility and getting the group on your side. Basically, you have to acknowledge and show empathy for their negative attitude toward your subject and the training, rather than take a superior attitude, force it upon them, or insist that it is the most important thing in the universe—which to them, it clearly is not.

More difficult to handle are audiences who are openly hostile and adversarial to the speaker. This is a situation you may never encounter as a businessperson who gives an occasional talk. But it can happen. The key to handling such hostility is keeping your cool. If your adversary is emotional, you remain logical and rational. If a critic insults you, do not respond in kind; take and keep the higher ground. You may think you are letting them get away with something. But the audience will soon empathize with you, support you (though they still may not agree with your point of view), and even defend you. Situations in which you may encounter a hostile audience:

1. Speaking to professionals whose industry is in a downturn or whose businesses are suffering because of a bad economy or recession, especially on a topic that does not directly help them cope with these problems, can be difficult.

2. Accountants and engineers are traditionally a difficult audience to please, although I do well with engineers because I am one.

3. Audiences going through major change—bankruptcy, divorce, illness, downsizing, mergers and acquisitions—are likely to be more irritable than attendees for whom the status quo is steady and peaceful.

4. When you or your topic are in opposition with the audience's beliefs; e.g., for an alternative healer speaking before a group of M.D.s at a medical college, the audience may not be receptive or cooperative.

5. Controversial topics are likely to draw more heat and criticism than informational topics.

6. Timing is also an important issue. Speeches scheduled at inopportune times—e.g., a training manager who schedules an interpersonal skills seminar for CPAs during tax season—may be inviting trouble.

"Everything God created has a kernel of excitement in it, as has everything civilization invented or discovered."
–Joseph J. Kelley, Jr.

Motivating Uncaring Attendees

Even talks that are mainly informative usually have a motivational element. It's needed because many of those in attendance are either bored by the topic or don't care about learning it, even if they are required to do so as part of their job. There are a couple of fixes for these conditions; let's start with boredom. Contrary to popular belief, technical or straightforward material is not inherently dull.

You need to find a kernel of excitement and get it to pop for your audience, using some of the presentation techniques outlined throughout this book. If your speech is boring, it is largely your fault, not the fault of the material you have been asked to present.

What about an indifferent audience? They are indifferent largely because they see no personal benefit in mastering the material. You must make the benefit clear to them. For instance, a manufacturer gave a training course on how to operate one of their machines. The course workbook began, "The Operator's Workstation acts as the interface between the Operator and the process being monitored and controlled. It is often referred to as the human interface to the process." This introduction fails on several fronts; it's impersonal, it's boring, and there's no incentive for the reader to want to learn what is being taught.

We rewrote the workbook introduction. The new opening began, "Your job is to monitor and control processes in your plant. Your operator's workstation can help you do that job better and faster, so your production line meets its target volume without you having to stay late or work a double shift." The new version is personal, more active and lively, and gives the reader an incentive to learn how to use the machine.

Speaking to Lay Audiences

When you are speaking to a lay audience about a complex, technical, or new subject, take extra care to be especially clear. Err on the side of pacing yourself too slowly rather than too quickly. In a half-day presentation or longer, stop near the end of each hour to review key points and answer any questions. Whenever you use jargon or a technical term, give a plain English definition and explanation of the term. Keep mathematics and equations to a minimum, and avoid them altogether if you can. Keep diagrams and graphics simple, and do not assume your audience can accurately interpret them on their own; walk them through schematics, flow charts, and the like step by step.

Lay audiences can be the easiest to please, provided the subject is interesting and the speaker is entertaining. But they are also the most easily bored. Tips to avoid boring the general public and keep them engaged:

◼ Get the audience actively involved in an exercise or activity.

Have Stories to Spare

"You should always have extra or reserve stories you are ready to add to your talk on the spot. There are four reasons why you might need them:

1. Participants sometimes ask for additional examples if they didn't get the point.

2. You sometimes unexpectedly find past participants sitting in the room who have heard your primary stories.

3. Even a proven story might not work.

4. One of your primary stories may be inappropriate for a particular audience."

—Alan Weiss, *Money Talks*

- Poll the audience by asking them questions; e.g., "How many people here drive a hybrid car?"

- Use motion, demonstrations, audio, and videos.

- Mix modes of presentation, e.g., first some lecture, than a group exercise, more lecture, a discussion, more lecture, a magic trick, lecture, group discussion. Mix it up.

- Start a friendly competition or contest and offer a prize to the winners.

Speaking to Experts

You may be asked to speak to audiences consisting of educated experts. You may think they know more than you do, and when it comes to knowledge of your company, product, industry, or field, some of your attendees may in fact have experience or knowledge that exceeds yours. But you don't have to worry about that, for two reasons.

First, they may have more general and broader knowledge of your specialty or discipline. But they do not have all the same experiences you do. They have theirs; you have yours. You as the speaker can and should learn from your audience. But no matter what their level of knowledge, they can learn from you. You know things that they do not.

For instance, one of my topics is direct mail marketing, a field in which you gain new knowledge and insight with every mailing you test. I frequently have people in the audience who have produced more mailings than I have. By the same token, I have conducted and seen the results of dozens of direct mail tests they haven't been told about. From these tests, I can illustrate principles, give tips, and demonstrate techniques in a way that enhances their knowledge.

The second reason why you need not fear speaking to an expert and knowledgeable audience is that these people, surprisingly, are often the most receptive and appreciative of the talks they attend. You might think that, because they are already pretty savvy in their disciplines, you can't tell them anything new. After all, they already know it all. But when they hear you teach things that they know and agree with, they benefit in several ways: It reinforces their knowledge; confirms what they already believe; reminds them of techniques they know but haven't tried lately; reawakens an interest in their field that may have waned; and of course, since your experience is not identical to theirs, they also get a new idea or two. There is an old saying, "School is never out for the pro," and it is the true professionals who seem to enjoy learning from seminars most. They will often approach the podium after your lecture with a smile, introduce themselves, shake your hand, and say, "You really know your stuff."

"Trust yourself. You know more than you think you do."
-Dr. Benjamin Spock

Speaking to a Mixed Audience

Some audiences are homogenous. Others are more diverse. What about an audience where knowledge levels and experience vary widely? Obviously, you want to avoid talking down to the experienced people, while not getting so technical that you leave the less knowledgeable attendees confused and frustrated. As a rule of thumb, though, it is better to err on the side of being too simple and explaining too much, than being too technical and assuming too much knowledge on the part of the listener. I have never heard a seminar attendee complain that the lecture was too clear or too easy to understand.

However, do not spend too much time on basics and fundamentals when speaking to a mixed audience. Instead, make available some reference materials in your handout that give quick reviews of basics. This way, the newbies in the audience can get up to speed at home, while the pros are not bored and don't feel your lecture is too elementary.

Mirroring: Tailoring Content, Pace, and Delivery

"Mirroring" means matching your tone, voice inflection, volume, vocabulary, speech patterns, even your accent to the people you are speaking with. Telemarketers, for instance, are taught to slow down when cold calling prospects in the south, and to talk rapidly when phoning potential customers in New York. The same mirroring technique works in conversations you have every day with customers, vendors, employees, business partners, and others you deal with. When someone seems hurried and distracted, I get right to the point and don't keep them on the phone. On the other hand, if a client clearly is relaxed, in a good mood, and wants to shoot the breeze, my conversation is more leisurely.

Mirroring can work in seminars, workshops, and meetings. If the crowd is somber, and your first few attempts at loosening them up don't work, avoid clowning and be business-like in manner and voice. Find something in common between you and your audience. For instance, if the event is being held at a resort hotel with a championship golf course and you golf, talk about golf. With experience, you'll improve your ability to adjust your talk in midstream to the mood, interests, and question from your audience. The more in synch you are with the other people in the room, the more they'll enjoy the experience.

Managing the Audience's Evaluation

I have mixed feelings about the technique I am about to give you for ensuring high ratings on your evaluation sheets. I know it works, and I used to do it routinely. But I haven't used it for years. Why not? Because I realized many years ago that the true measure of a speaker's success is not the evaluations or applause or standing ovation, but hearing from students a month or a year or 10 years after the class, telling you how much what you taught them changed

Speaking for Results

"Every speech should have an outcome—results appropriate to the topic and the environment. The more distinct and enduring the outcomes, the greater the probability that you will be both rehired and referred to others. Standing ovations don't last longer than a minute and don't increase your fee by one cent."

—Alan Weiss, *Money Talks*

your life. As I mentioned earler, I have several students who still stay in touch with me more than 20 years after they attended one of my workshops!

Still, I realize for many who speak, getting good evaluations is important. So here is a technique that was taught to me by Dr. Rob Gilbert (and modified slightly) that you can use to virtually ensure high marks. Ideally, it works best if the students have a pen and pencil and an index card. I bring index cards to make sure they do, and hand them out when I am ready to implement the technique.

About three-quarters of the way through your talk, pause, and as you hand out index cards, say to the class, "Take out a pen. Rate this talk on a scale of 1 to 10. One is awful, 10 is terrific. Write down your rating on the index card in front of you. Don't show it to me." After they comply, continue, "Now, if you did not rate this class an 8, 9, or 10, think about the one thing I would have to tell you that would make it an 8, 9, or 10, and clearly write that down on your card."

Once they have finished, collect the cards. Either now or a bit later, begin going through the cards. Briefly answer every question or address every item on the cards or as many of them as time allows. When you do this, the majority of your evaluations will be high. Why? For those who had a specific point they wanted you to cover, you've done that. For those who didn't write down anything, they will think, "Well, he asked me what he needed to do to get a good rating, and I didn't answer him, so to be fair, I have to give him a good evaluation." It's a pure gimmick, but it works. And it also does help ensure that you cover what these attendees really wanted to learn.

Post-Seminar Support

Increasingly, speakers, seminar companies, trainers, and other providers of adult education offer post-seminar resources where attendees can continue their learning. Today, the most common is to maintain a content-rich website on your speaking topic, and refer attendees there for more information. Ideally, the website is not static but dynamic, with new content added frequently. Other post-seminar learning opportunities you can offer your audiences include an online forum, your blog, webinars, podcasts, tele-seminars, e-classes, and online newsletters. You can give attendees a password to access the clients-only segments of your content-rich website. Or, you can deliver

Write and publish a monthly online newsletter on your area of expertise. Offer a free subscription as a value-added bonus to your attendees whenever you speak.

the post-seminar follow-up content by e-mail, which requires attendees to give you their e-mail address. When you e-mail materials to past seminar attendees, you must always include a mechanism in your e-mail they can use to have their name removed from your list if they no longer want to receive your e-mail content.

Your web-based content can be free to everyone; or a portion may be password-protected, and seminar attendees given access with a password that expires in 30, 60, or 90 days after the event. An alternative is to create a paid membership website for your content, with a monthly subscription fee of $29 to $99 or more. You then include a free month's membership for your workshop attendees. They see that you actually do charge others to access the content, which creates a high perceived value of the post-seminar support.

Covering Everything the Audience Wants to Know

Here is a review of the techniques you can use to ensure that your presentation covers the important points your audience wants you to teach them:

1. Have the meeting planner complete and return your Pre-Program Questionnaire (see Appendix II).

2. Have attendees complete and return your Attendee Audit Form to you (see Appendix IV).

3. Interview the meeting planner and a few of the potential attendees over the phone prior to the presentation.

4. Walk around the room prior to beginning your presentation and speak to the early arrivers about what they want to learn.

5. Go around the room at the start of your talk and ask each attendee to tell you the one thing they want to get out of your speech.

6. Give out index cards in the middle of your program and ask the attendees to write down the one thing they absolutely want you to cover that you have not yet covered.

7. Have a strong handout that summarizes the content in your presentation and also contains additional content you may not have had time to cover during your talk.

8. Give attendees post-seminar access to additional study materials on your topic.

The lobster family reunion gone terribly wrong.

Know who is coming to your event
so you can relate well to them.

CHAPTER 10

Presentation Tips for Special Situations

Know just what to say - and how to say it - for every occasion that you are asked to speak.

This chapter gives quick and specific tips for a variety of speakers facing different speaking challenges, including:

- Workplace presentations
- Corporate training
- Shareholder meetings
- Analyst briefings
- Elementary and high school students
- Orals for graduate students
- Adult education
- Toasts and roasts
- Sermons

- Eulogies

- Keynotes

- Break-out sessions

- Roundtables

- Panels

- Tele-seminars

- Webinars

- Town meetings

- Clubs and fraternal organizations

Workplace Presentations

The corporate culture at your workplace largely dictates the manner and style of presentations given in the workplace. For example, many Fortune 500 managers who give talks use, in my view, overly elaborate and complex PowerPoint presentations. They usually have too many slides (violating the one slide per minute rule) with print too small to read. Great pains have been taken to ensure consistent format among all the slides in the presentation.

At the other end of the spectrum, small entrepreneurial companies are more informal in their workplace meetings and presentations. They may use PowerPoint slides, but do so to make ideas clear, not impress others in the room with how good they are at using PowerPoint.

In a small workplace meeting (a dozen attendees or fewer) in which not everyone knows everyone else, start by going around the room. Ask each person to briefly say their name, title, department, and interest in or involvement with the topic of the presentation.

If you are the speaker and you know several of the people in the room, refer to them, their work, and their ideas during your presentation, e.g., "Bill and I were looking at this just the other day; let me share with you his suggestions, which I think are excellent." Give credit where credit is due. Do not try to make it seem like every accomplishment and idea is yours, even if they are. Go out of your way to flatter, in a genuine manner, your coworkers and colleagues; it will win them over and make them feel good about themselves all day long.

Workplace presentations are perhaps the most informal venue for speakers. Yet you do have to follow some of the key principles of good public speaking, even here. These include clarity, accuracy, brevity, specificity, and utility. Is your presentation easy for people to understand? Don't be obscure or overly technical, thinking that you are speaking to a group who knows everything you do; nobody knows everything you do. Your coworkers are busy and meetings are a tremendous drain on their time, so don't drone on and on—get to the point. By "utility," I mean make sure what you tell them is useful; present information that helps them do their jobs better and enables the organization to meet its objectives.

Association Meetings

For most businesspeople speaking at association meetings, the goal is to publicize their company, promote their product, and—even more desirable—generate qualified sales leads. To make this happen, you must have a handout. The handout is typically an outline, article reprint, white paper, or hard copy of your PowerPoint presentation. You can bring enough copies of the handout for every attendee, or you can invite them to ask you for it and then send it to them after your talk. There are pros and cons to both methods, but the latter is the best way to generate inquiries from your presentation.

An effective method of distributing handouts is the "green sheet" method. It maximizes the number of attendees who take handouts, increases their desire to have the material, and importantly, eliminates any hint of self-promotion or salesmanship. Here's how it works: Prepare a handout that expands

How to Really Connect With Your Audience

"Speakers should attend the entire event, if possible. Speakers can get to know the attendees better by being accessible throughout the event. If there is a luncheon or dinner, sit at a table with attendees, not with the other speakers. When speakers sit together at one table, they create the impression of an old boys club that is unapproachable and aloof."

—Bret Ridgeway, *View from the Back*

on one of the points in your talk, covering it in more detail than you can in a short presentation. Or make the handout a supplement, covering additional points not discussed but related to the topic.

Another option is to do a handout that's a resource guide; for example, a bibliography of reference books on your topic, tables of technical data, a glossary of key terms, a series of equations or examples of calculations, and the like. The important point is that the handout relates to *but does not merely repeat* information covered in your talk; instead, it *expands* on it. And, even more importantly, print it on green paper. You'll see why in a second.

When you get to that topic in your talk, which should be about halfway or three-quarters through the presentation, discuss the point, then say something similar to the following (adapting it to your topic and handout, of course), "I really can't cover in this short talk all of the techniques related to this, so I've prepared a checklist of 25 points to consider when planning this type of project, and reprinted it on this *green sheet*." Pause, hold up the sheet for everyone to see, then continue, "I have plenty of copies, so if you want one, come up to me after the talk and I'll give you a copy."

After your talk, you will be surrounded at the podium by a large crowd of people with their hands out to get the free green sheet. Try it—it works. Oh, and why a "green sheet" rather than copying it on plain white paper?

Doing it on colored paper and calling it a green sheet just seems to make it more special; also, instead of having to remember what's actually in the sheet (many people would not and therefore would hesitate to ask for it), people can just come up and say, "May I have a green sheet, please?"

Let's say the conference organizer will not release a list of attendees or those who go to your specific session, but you want to capture as many of those names as possible for marketing follow-up. In that case, offer your handout as a bait piece—something the attendee must request that you will deliver later—rather than giving it out at the session. At the conclusion of your talk, discuss your handout and what it covers, and say, "So if you would like a free copy of our free telecom security checklist, just write 'TSC' on the back of your business card and hand it to me. I'll e-mail a free copy of the checklist to you as soon as I get back to the office." The more enticing and relevant your bait piece, the more business cards you will collect. A really strong bait-piece offer can get you the business cards of 25 to 75 percent of attendees or more.

You can offer to e-mail your PowerPoint to anyone who gives you their business card. At many conferences, your PowerPoint slides are reprinted in a conference workbook given to attendees, but the slides are usually reduced in size to fit three or four slides per page instead of one per page. When that happens, I tell attendees, "My PowerPoint slides are in your conference book, but at that size, they're a little difficult to read. If you'd like, give me your business card and I will e-mail you a copy of the PowerPoint file so you can print them out full size." A large percentage of attendees will take you up on this offer.

Product Seminars

A promotional or product seminar, one designed ultimately to sell a product or service rather than be a profit center in itself, helps move consumers one step closer to a purchase decision. It does so by providing the knowledge consumers feel they need to make an intelligent buying decision.

Unlike a tutorial, which is more of a pure informational seminar with the pitch for the service limited to the beginning, the end, and the coffee breaks, a product seminar usually combines advice on how to do something (such as how to stay fit and trim) with a lengthy demonstration of a specific product (how to use Brand X rowing machine). The length of the program is typically two or three hours. For groups of business prospects, breakfast is usually provided at morning seminars; lunch at afternoon programs. Evening sessions are usually followed by an open bar and light snacks.

Seminars help promote products and services in three ways: By establishing the seminar giver as the authority, demonstrating the product, and "setting the specs" for a product purchase. "Show your prospect that the ideal product conforms to a list of very specific criteria," says advertising executive Bruce J. Bloom. "Then you prove that your product meets each of those criteria." As Bloom explains, the trick is to work backward. First, identify the major strengths of your product and its competitive advantages over other products in its category. Then, develop a checklist of product selection criteria that conforms to all of your product's strengths and advantages.

"When your prospect accepts your criteria, it becomes far easier to persuade him to accept your product," concludes Bloom. There are two reasons why this is so. First, your product fits the criteria he now accepts better than any other product on the market. Second, just the very act of publishing the selection criteria positions you and your firm as the knowledgeable experts in this area; people almost always prefer to do business with the top experts in any given discipline or field.

Corporate Training

As defined in Chapter 1, corporate training refers to classes held on site at a company to teach their employees skills useful in the workplace. Topics can range from soft skills such as time management and leadership to hard skills such as engine repair or data warehousing.

Dr. Gary Blake of The Communication Workshop, a corporate training firm specializing in writing skills for insurance claims adjusters, offers the fol-

lowing suggestions for presenting corporate training programs:

Don't take yourself too seriously when doing corporate training. Often, attendees were forced to go, aren't interested in your topic, and resent being there. A light-hearted approach can diffuse hostility and enhance learning.

1. *Over-prepare.* "I always have more handouts
    than I need," says Gary. "I am ready with an
    extra layer of knowledge about what I am dis-
    cussing so that if a person inquires about serial
    commas or who and whom, I am ready with
    examples."

2. *Keep changing the game.* Blake plans surprises
    throughout his seminars. First, he gives atten-
    dees writing samples to critique, then individ-
    ual exercises, then group exercises. At the end
    of the class, he takes out a $5 bill and bets the
    class that they won't be able to spell three
    words correctly. "I save 'supersede' for the third and lose my five dollars
    only once in every 40 seminars," he says.

3. *Have a good opening.* "At the beginning of the seminar, I like to make a
    humorous reference to the seminar's locale, a well-known restaurant,
    recent news, weather, just to let people know that humor will be a part
    of the day," says Gary.

4. *End humorously.* "I have, for many years, ended by quoting the words of
    that immortal Californian, Porky Pig: 'That's all folks.' As I say the words,
    I give a final wave of my hand while simultaneously closing my note-
    book. Leave 'em laughing."

5. *Be attentive.* Nancy Reagan had "the stare," but you don't have to go that
    far. Just look at each person who asks a question, nod your head, look at
    them, and then, in your answer, mention their name by saying, "Tom,
    that's a great question...."

Shareholder Meetings

As the name implies, your audience at shareholder meetings is primarily individuals as well as institutional investors who hold shares of your company's stock. Anyone may attend, though management is often focused on communicating with the institutional and wealthy individual shareholders who hold large positions in the stock. Objectives can vary. One is to outline business and financial progress for the most recent quarter or year, as well as plans and forecasts for the coming quarter or year. Another is to convey the most positive picture of business and financial health possible, so that shareholders won't dump the stock and, if anything, will be motivated to acquire more shares.

Shareholder meetings can be raucous affairs, especially if an outspoken shareholder is in the audience mercilessly grilling the CEO of a company whose shares have taken a nosedive. On the other hand, the manner in which you conduct shareholder meetings must conform with Securities & Exchange

The Importance of Staying in Character

"One hundred percent of the time I stay in the persona I want to convey to the audience," says speaker Paul Hartunian. "With my publicity talk, that persona is 'I'm one of you. I tried a lot of things, then hit the jackpot with this one idea. This is the formula I used that you can model.' I truly want the people in the audience to get that, and to understand that they have the same chance to hit it big. My audiences always say that it was clear to them that I truly cared about their success, instead of just yapping about mine. Most importantly, I'm for real. I'm just a guy up there telling his story, the way it really happened."

Commission (SEC) requirements. In addition to the SEC guidelines, individual states often have additional requirements for conducting shareholder meetings. Consult your corporate counsel on how to comply with both SEC and state regulations. Most publicly traded companies are required to hold at least one shareholder meeting a year.

Analyst Briefings

Both shareholder meetings and analyst briefings communicate information on publicly traded companies. But while shareholder meetings focus on the shareholder, analyst meetings bring professional stock analysts up to date on a publicly traded company they are or may be following. Analyst briefings may be given by the company's director of investor relations, public relations manager, CFO, or CEO, depending in the size of the business. The goal is to portray a favorable picture of the company so that analysts conclude that owning the stock is a good investment, and write favorable reports promoting the stock to their brokerage's stockbrokers and clients.

If you are going to write or give briefings to analysts, you must acquire a working knowledge of the business whose stock you are promoting as well as of how the stock market works. Analysts understand the market, or believe they do. But often, they don't grasp the business model that drives your company. If you can show them how the business makes money, why it is likely to make even more money in the future, and the reasons why the company has a sustainable competitive advantage in its marketplace, analysts will be more likely to write a favorable report.

Your main mission is to communicate this story in a clear, compelling way. Analysts buy into stories, and further, they know that individual investors buy into stories, too. They are looking for a good story to tell in the research report they are writing about your stock. Feed them that story, prove it, make it credible, and they will feed it to their sales team and clients.

Elementary and High School Students

From the early grades through high school and college, students are occasionally—though perhaps not as frequently as they should be—required to stand up in front of the class and give an oral presentation. Oral presentations have been required in schools for centuries. What is different about them today? Surprisingly, or perhaps not so surprisingly, the emphasis today is on putting together great graphics and visuals in support of the oral presentation.

When I went to elementary school in the 1960s, we created our graphics using markers and poster-sized cardboard sheets. Since most of us could not draw well, the focus was on the content of your presentation, not the oral delivery or the graphics. Our visuals were crudely hand-drawn, and for the most part looked it. A minority of students then spent endless hours making "pretty" presentations; e.g., using stenciling instead of hand-drawn letters.

My sons did some projects with poster boards and marketers. But they were also required to create PowerPoint presentations. Children think the main point is to learn the subject matter of the presentation; e.g., American history, the environment, the weather. But in reality, they are being trained in the more important skill of creating and giving presentations. In his book *Talking to an Audience* (Sterling Publishing, 1963), Vernon Howard offers the following tips to schoolchildren who want to master public speaking:

1. Speak in a natural manner. Give a simple and sincere talk.

2. Talk to the listeners just as you talk with friends. Your hearers are your friends.

3. For classroom fun, talk about an odd subject. It's fun for everyone.

4. Don't apologize for mistakes. Correct them as best you can, then continue.

5. Be a leader. Take charge of your audience from the very start.

Teachers

If you are a teacher, then teaching and speaking in front of a group—your class—is something you do on a daily basis. During grades K–12, great teachers immediately focus on getting control of their classroom in the first few days. It's essential so that you can spend the rest of the year teaching. There will be some years you are blessed with well-behaved, eager-to-learn classes; there will be as many years of classrooms filled with potential chaos.

Many teachers have lots of rules. But according to former special education teacher Fern Dickey, you really only need three rules, and they're easy for pupils to remember: Raise your hand for permission to speak, remain in your seat, and when the teacher turns the lights out, immediately return to your seats if you are standing or walking around for a special group projects. During the first few weeks of schools, practice and reinforce these rules until they are second nature. Once you have control of the class, the year will be a great one for you and your students.

Lessons should have elements of different types of learning components. "Too often, sadly, we still teach our kids the way we did during the Industrial Revolution," says Fern. "Teaching should encompass all aspects of how the human mind learns." Rafe Esquith, a fifth grade teacher at the Hobart Boulevard Elementary School in Los Angeles, epitomizes this. His book, *Teach Like Your Hair's On Fire: The Methods and Madness Inside Room 56,* shows teachers how to successfully motivate and teach a classroom of children, all of whom are operating at different learning levels.

Almost universally, kids like teachers who have a sense of humor better than teachers who present themselves as aloof and rigid authority figures.

Ongoing assessment is key. As the saying goes in business, you can't manage what you can't measure, and the same is true with your students. This doesn't mean the standardized tests, which Dickey sees as a necessary evil. Teachers should always be evaluating pupils to see where more help is needed.

Orals for Graduate Students

In an oral exam, a graduate student, a candidate for either a Masters degree or a Ph.D., must explain his thesis to an academic committee and answer their questions about it. When the thesis is accepted and the student passes his orals, he is granted the degree.

Pat Cryer, an honorary professor at the University of Winchester, offers the following tips for doing well on your oral examination:

1. Reread your thesis just a few days before the date of your oral examination to refresh your memory and understanding of its contents.

2. Use Post-It notes or paper clips to mark key areas of your thesis that the committee may ask you to discuss so you can find them quickly.

3. Bring with you your thesis, a pen and paper, and a box of tissues in case you sweat or anxiety causes your eyes to tear up a bit.

Cutting Your Presentation Short

You may have prepared extensively to deliver your one-hour presentation, only to discover in horror that the meeting is running late and you are being given just ten minutes. Don't complain or give the meeting planner grief. Step up, do your ten minutes pleasantly, thank the audience, and end on time. Both the meeting planner and the audience will appreciate your flexibility, graciousness, and brevity.

4. Sit up straight and look at the members of the committee, so your body language shows you are listening to their comments and questions.

5. If you are not sure you understand the question or that you have answered it in a way that is satisfactory to them, ask for clarification.

6. Be prepared to defend your major points. Be prepared to concede a few minor points, but not too many.

7. If an examiner makes a valid criticism, acknowledge that you agree with them. You can admit that you hadn't thought about the point before, but better is to say you hope that other researchers will do more work on that particular point.

Adult Education

By adult education, also known as *continuing education,* we mean teaching adult learners. Seminar companies, colleges, high schools, YMCAs, and other institutions all have adult education classes or programs. The students are grown-ups, not kids, and therein you'll find the difference. With children in elementary, junior high, and high school, their primary job is to go to school and get an education, and the teacher is the authority in charge. College is similar, except college students are there voluntarily and paying a lot of money to attend, whereas public school students are required by law to attend until age 16 or so (in most states).

As an advertisement for Saint Peter's College states, "Adult students have unique needs." Adults taking continuing education classes are also there voluntarily and are paying you to teach them. But unless like most college students, whose major activity is learning, the majority activity of most of the adults in your class is working and earning a living. They already have a full-time job, and therefore school is an extra burden on top of that. They may also have many other responsibilities, from coaching Little League and making monthly mortgage payments, to lawn care and home maintenance. As an adult education instructor, you must show respect for the students, who are sacrificing free time and hard-earned money to be there. You must treat them more as peers, less like your charges. You can still give homework assignments in adult education classes, but the amount of homework must be light, with each assignment taking no more than an hour or so per week.

Toasts

A toast involves making a brief comment over drinks at a wedding, anniversary party, Bar Mitzvah, christening, or similar event. It's literally a few sentences and should take seconds—certainly no more than a minute—to deliver. Toasts should be kind and sincere. Many people giving a toast feel pressure to be clever, funny, or original, and agonize over preparation of their remarks. The easiest approach, and one that always goes over well, is to tell a touching, warm, nice story about the person or couple being toasted that portrays them in a good light, is not embarrassing or a violation of their privacy in any way, and that most of the people in the room haven't heard before.

Roasts

Roasts are banquets or dinners where a guest of honor is subject both to praise as well as humorous barbs by associates or colleagues. A roast can be a very effective way of bringing any company, association, or fraternal organization much closer together. On the other hand, a roast can wreak havoc and cause irreparable damage if executed with poor judgment.

There are two basic types of roasts. The Friar's Roast is the one you see on Comedy Central. Hosts such as Jeff Ross and guest roasters like Lisa Lampanelli are there to make fun of the person being roasted. Their goals are pure entertainment as well as to create a shock effect with the studio and TV audience.

These roasts are uncensored, bawdy, tasteless, edgy to the point of downright ridicule, and yes, quite funny. The more the guest of honor is embarrassed and squirms at the outrageous jokes, the funnier it gets. The guests know what they are getting into when they agree to be on the show. But the guest of honor at your roast may not.

Now, the other roast kind that you'll remember seeing as a kid (if you're a baby-boomer) was the Dean Martin Celebrity Roasts. "Dino" did them with his crew of funny cronies such as Sammy Davis, Jr., Don Rickles, and Muhammad Ali. These gems (that still hold up today if you're lucky to view them) were also done with a cutting edge, but the knife is dulled and applied with much love and admiration for the guest of honor—and in good humor (the material was also censored for network TV). This is the type of roast that you should strive to put on.

Here are four important aspects to remember when being on the dais and delivering material at a roast—so you don't get burned:

1. *Humor is subjective.* What you think is funny to your co-workers (if you all share the same info) might not go over with the CEO or your superior you've been asked to "roast." The boss might be a good sport. But she does not want to ridiculed, downright insulted, or made to look like a fool to the rank and file.

2. *Use humor based on truth.* The truth shall set you free. It's also very, very, funny when presented the right way to your audience, as long as they all share the same knowledge about the person. When creating jokes about the guest of honor, remember to get to the lowest common denominator, which is the essence of that person's quirkiness; e.g., if the roastee is cheap and everyone knows it, that's a theme you should focus on.

If you genuinely dislike someone, decline an invitation to be one of his roasters. Your animosity will come through and make you look bad.

3. *When in doubt, leave it out.* You have a wonderful, acerbic joke about the guest of honor that

you know will kill the audience. But if you know it will embarrass the guest of honor to the point where it does damage, leave it out. For instance, if the guest of honor is married and is known to be a womanizer, that is not a good arena to venture into. Don Imus found out the hard way when delivering a speech about Bill Clinton's philandering and Hillary was on the dais. The audience felt empathy for Hillary and quickly turned on Imus after he made the remark.

4. *Pick your targets carefully.* For the most part, the guest of honor is (he hopes) held in high regard within his company, and by his friends and family that are present. If you're downright insulting without being funny, or if the joke "crosses the line," your audience will mumble and boo. And the next day at the office when your superior comes up to you he might say to you, "Why in God's name did you choose that joke?"

Your boss will have a long memory, especially when your work comes up for review. Always get the chairperson in charge of the roast to sign-off on your material. Also, go over your jokes with other "roastees" to make sure you're not repeating the exact subject matter. There's nothing worse than delivering a joke similar to one that was done a few minutes ago and getting no response from your audience.

Have a great time at the roast. Launch your barbs with love, affection, and good intentions; that way, your audience and your guest of honor will appreciate your efforts.

Sermons

Sermons are written and delivered primarily by pastors and secondarily by lay speakers invited to be a guest sermonizer at the pulpit on Sunday. Sermons usually combine some or all of the following elements: quotes from the scriptures; retelling of a Biblical tale; personal anecdotes from the minister's life; stories about church members (preferably not naming or identifying them in any way without their permission) or other people well known to the congregation; advice, rules, recommendations, principles, or instructions on how to live a good, happy, and productive life; observations and commentary on news, politics, and current events linked to a lesson; and a call to action (e.g., attending church more frequently, contributing to the community, helping stop kids from experimenting with drugs, or convincing their children to abstain from pre-marital sex).

Within this combination of elements, the sermon can span a spectrum from focusing on practical life issues of personal importance to the congregation to a strict interpretation and reading of the Bible. "If the audience is a congregation of newly married couples, a topical sermon on how to foster a closer relationship with a spouse would be appropriate," writes Marcus Peterson. "If the congregation is a general one that needs to just hear the Word of God, an expository sermon is all right."

Eulogies

When you give a eulogy, you are not the center of attention—the deceased is. The audience consists of people who knew the deceased, such as business associates, acquaintances, neighbors, friends, relatives, children, grandchildren, siblings, and spouse or partner. The purpose of the eulogy is to mark the departed's passing and give comfort to those left behind.

Even eulogies, though, work best when you follow the rules of public speaking laid out in this book. The main rule in this case is to put the audience first. So when I stood up to deliver the eulogy at my father's funeral, I began this way: "Everyone wants to be happy. Is there anyone here who does not want to be happy?" I had their attention, and continued, "Dave Bly knew the secret of happiness, and in a minute, I'm going to reveal it to you." I then told a few stories of how my father loved to entertain people with jokes, magic tricks, humor, and especially with kids, to help them.

The secret to happiness and a good life, I concluded, is to make others happy, which is what my father did. I explained that people who had met him

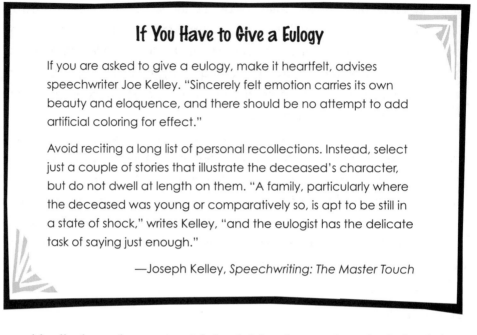

If You Have to Give a Eulogy

If you are asked to give a eulogy, make it heartfelt, advises speechwriter Joe Kelley. "Sincerely felt emotion carries its own beauty and eloquence, and there should be no attempt to add artificial coloring for effect."

Avoid reciting a long list of personal recollections. Instead, select just a couple of stories that illustrate the deceased's character, but do not dwell at length on them. "A family, particularly where the deceased was young or comparatively so, is apt to be still in a state of shock," writes Kelley, "and the eulogist has the delicate task of saying just enough."

—Joseph Kelley, *Speechwriting: The Master Touch*

would talk about the magic trick he did for them or how he helped them properly bait their hook and catch a fish—he loved fishing and was always helping kids catch a little sunfish or bass. They would remember the incident decades from now, thus making Dad live on in their memories.

Keynotes

At national meetings of associations and large corporations, the keynote is the most important speech. Everyone is invited into a large ballroom to hear the keynote speaker, who typically speaks for about an hour. The keynote may be delivered first thing in the morning or at the luncheon on first day of the event. Keynotes are often given by celebrities, industry big shots, or top professional speakers. Where other speakers who handle "breakout sessions" (see page 199) deliver practical instruction and a high level of content, the keynote is expected to be more dynamic, entertaining, and stirring.

Breakout Sessions

The breakout sessions at a conference or meetings are those lectures given by speakers other than the keynote speaker. The breakout sessions may be sequential (a single talk to all attendees in one large room, followed in series by other single-speaker talks in the same room) or concurrent (simultaneous talks by multiple speakers in different rooms, with the attendees given the option to choose the talk they want to attend).

One of the special challenges of giving a breakout session at a conference is determining when exactly to begin. Though you may be scheduled to start at 10am after the keynote is finished, you don't know when the keynote is over. The attendees are in the main ballroom listening to the keynote. But you don't hear it, because you're preparing for your talk in a separate, smaller room designated specifically for your session.

Often, either due to lack of vigilance on the part of the meeting planner or keynote speaker or both, the keynote speech runs long. I've also seen meeting schedules where the keynote is scheduled to end at 10 A.M., and the first breakout sessions to begin at 10 A.M. The logistics of this are impossible, unless the attendees can teleport out of the main ballroom into your room. Of course, they cannot, and it takes several minutes between sessions for attendees to decide which breakout seminar they want to attend (they often change their minds or leave the decision until the last minute).

Roundtables

Another type of presentation you may encounter at conferences and association meetings is the roundtable, named after the round tables used for conducting the sessions. In a typical roundtable session, there are multiple tables. Each has a sign indicating the topic to be covered at that table, and each table is assigned a specific speaker, member, or expert as the leader. The number of different topics/tables typically ranges from 5 to 15, depending on the size of

the event. The roundtable session typically lasts an hour, during which attendees can attend three 20-minute roundtables. Up to a dozen or more attendees plus the presenter can be seated at each table at one time.

A roundtable is not a lecture; it is a small group discussion of which you
(as the presenter) are the facilitator. In a 20-minute roundtable, I recommend
spending the time as follows:

- The leader welcomes the group to the roundtable. She introduces herself and the topic of the session.

- Going around the table, attendees state their name, company, and job
  title.

- The leader spends five minutes or so giving some useful content relating to the topic.

- She then opens the session up for discussion, which she facilitates.

The leader is not expected to answer all the questions and issues raised. A better approach, when a question is asked, is to encourage other people in the
group to chime in and share their experiences. A roundtable does not require
a handout, but I suggest bringing one. That way, the attendees leave with a
piece of paper that contains not only valuable tips but also your name and contact information.

Panels

A panel is a breakout session, usually an hour long. But instead of a presentation by a single speaker, there are shorter presentations by multiple
panel members. There is a moderator who welcomes the attendees, introduces the panelists, and facilitates the session. In addition to the moderator,
there are either three or four subject matter experts on the panel, with the
time divided evenly between them. Therefore, in an hour-long panel session
with three panelists, each has about 20 minutes to speak. Although not

required to do so, panelists would be wise to get together for a short conference call prior to the event. The main purpose of this pre-panel call is to ensure that the presentations are complementary and not redundant.

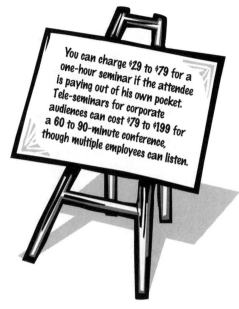

You can charge $29 to $79 for a one-hour seminar if the attendee is paying out of his own pocket. Tele-seminars for corporate audiences can cost $79 to $199 for a 60 to 90-minute conference, though multiple employees can listen.

Tele-seminars

A tele-seminar is a seminar, speech, or other educational information delivered to a group on the phone via a shared conference line. The presenter is in what is called "lecture mode" and is the only one who can talk for most of the program; the other people on the call, the audience, can just listen. On some calls, a moderator takes questions from callers who can be selected to speak by pressing a key on their phone as instructed by the moderator. Usually the presentation, including the question-and-answer period, is 60 to 90 minutes in length.

There are many benefits to presenting tele-seminars as opposed to live seminars. The speaker and attendees need not travel; students can take the tele-seminar without leaving their desks. No internet connection or PC is required; all you need is a telephone. The audio conference services providing the bridge lines for the event can record the audio conference, and many will send you a transcription for a small extra fee.

Tele-seminars are also a relatively inexpensive way to "practice" your material, providing you with an audience and feedback; attendees ask questions during the tele-seminar over the phone, and afterward, via e-mail.

Tele-seminars are used by individuals like you and me, as well as major companies and associations. These groups often have a series of tele-seminars, which is something you could consider doing if your topic is too large for a one-time presentation.

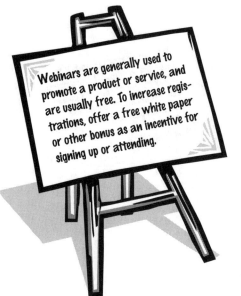

Webinars are generally used to promote a product or service, and are usually free. To increase registrations, offer a free white paper or other bonus as an incentive for signing up or attending.

Webinars

A webinar is essentially a tele-seminar with a visual component added. The visual material is delivered to the attendees to their PC desktops over the internet. The visuals can be a static PowerPoint, a dynamic PowerPoint that the seminar moderator or presenter controls, or even a live software demo. For some reason, tele-seminars have become the preferred format for associations offering educational programs to their members, while corporations use free webinars mainly as a sales tool. Webinars seem better suited to situations where attendees participate in their offices and each has access to his own phone and PC. With a tele-seminar, multiple attendees at a single company can listen by placing the call on a speakerphone in a conference room.

Podcasts

A podcast is an audio file that you create in MP3 format. The file is uploaded to your server and distributed via e-mail to your target audience, who downloads the MP3 either to their computer or mobile device. They can then listen to it at their leisure. These podcasts combine a number of technologies that allow listeners to "subscribe" to audio files online to play back on their personal audio player (iPod and such) or computer.

The ideal length of a podcast is 10 minutes to 20 minutes. If you go more than 25 minutes, you're outside the average commute or past the average treadmill workout. The podcast should be broken up into short segments, as it can get boring hearing the same announcer speaking away for 20 solid minutes. Many corporate podcasters edit their audio file into multiple segments of three to five minutes each.

Although it's fine to outline your podcast in detail, too much editing causes a loss of spontaneity, which can turn the audience off. Rob Walch, in *Tricks of the Podcasting Masters* (Que, 2006), advises you use body language to keep your vocal energy high. So for maximum impact when you record your podcast, get up and walk around, smile, gesture, or do whatever you normally do when you're deep in conversation. Modulate your voice; put feeling and emotion into your words. Pretend you're talking to your best friend to help you with a lively delivery. Stand up instead of staying seated. Or take a walk in the park.

Choose your podcast title carefully. Remember, you're competing with tens of thousands of other podcasts to catch the interest of podcast browsers searching directories for something related to their current interest or conundrum. Pick a name for your podcast that closely matches your content topic. What should the title be? While your podcast name can have your company or brand name in it, you should also consider a secondary name. Don't call it "My Corporation Podcast Issue I," which is truly a recipe for boring. You're trying to build a brand relationship with the audience over time, so incorporating your brand as a component of your title makes sense.

Town Meetings

Whether you are a town official speaking from the platform or a citizen speaking from the floor, be aware that town meetings are often contentious. The town has to justify an action it plans to take or has already taken to a group of people who oppose it. If you are a citizen fighting city hall and yours is a minority position, recruit any allies you can find and get them to attend the meeting with you; there is strength in numbers. Think about how the town is likely to defend their position or counter your arguments, and be prepared with a response. Research the issue prior to the meeting so you come armed with as many facts as possible. When you state them, cite the source. Even better, bring the documents with you, especially photographs.

Clubs and Fraternal Organizations

The Rotary, the Elks Club, B'nai B'rith, and other fraternal organizations often have guest speakers at their lunch and dinner meetings. Often, the speaker is there to entertain, to raise funds, to support or plead for a cause, or to educate the audience on a subject of importance to them. These groups seldom pay speakers, so they are a good opportunity to practice your presentation skills in a venue where performance is not critical and the stakes are not high (if you're not getting paid, they don't expect you to be great).

Professional Speakers

If you are a professional speaker, I urge you to ignore most of the advice you get on making presentations from other professional speakers. Do not cultivate the theatrical or dramatic mannerisms or the clichéd ideas and themes that so many professional speakers seem to embrace. Be a high-content speaker who is also clear, empathetic, and engaging. Your greatest reward should be attendees telling you a month or a year after your presentation that what you told them improved their lives, not high marks on your evaluation sheets or a standing ovation, nice as both of those are.

What Now?

There is one more secret to improving your presentation skills that I didn't want to reveal early in the book because I feared it might discourage you. But now that you have a step-by-step roadmap to becoming a more effective speaker, I want to close with this secret.

The secret, which I think you probably already know deep down, is that you can't become a great or even competent speaker merely by taking a class or reading a book. Those things can help, but the only way to improve your public speaking skills is through repetition, practice, and experience.

The first time you give a talk is going to be the worst time. The second time will be better, and the 100th time much better. There are many skills in this life that are mostly mastered by doing rather than studying, and public speaking is certainly one of them.

A common piece of advice given to aspiring professional speakers is to speak at small engagements for free to hone their skills. Then, only when they are competent, should they accept a speaking engagement for pay.

Even if you are not a professional speaker, this approach makes sense. Speak whenever you can, wherever you can, but especially at venues where the expectations are low and your performance is not critical. One of the best opportunities is to be the lay speaker at your church, either reading the week's Bible selection or delivering the lay sermon. One of the most valuable functions Toastmasters provides for its members is the opportunity to practice speaking in front of a live audience in a setting where a poor performance does not adversely affect you. After Toastmasters, you might step up to an evening lecture at the local library or a lunch talk to local businesspeople at the chamber of commerce. If you are an author with a recently published book, the Barnes & Noble in your town would probably like to have you speak one evening.

When you start out speaking in public, begin with short presentations. Many of the first exercises you do in Toastmasters are literally just two or three minutes. Why is this important? Because the instant you start a two- or three-minute speech, the end is already near. Shorter talks are less anxiety provoking for beginning speakers. Conversely, the longer the talk, the more difficult it is to present, because the longer you must sustain the audience's attention and interest. Once you have mastered the three-minute talk, move up next to a ten-minute presentation at a local club meeting, then a 20-minute lunch talk. Then you will be ready for a 45-minute workshop or three-hour training session.

Should you give the same talk repeatedly or vary your presentations? There are advantages to both. When you give a talk repeatedly, you become more comfortable with it and, without deliberately doing so, actually memorize all or most of it. I discovered this in high school when I played in the orchestra for the school play, a musical, *Bye Bye Birdy.* Even though I was in the orchestra, and not an actor in the play, within a week or so I, and everyone in the orchestra, realized we knew all or most of the lines in the play by heart.

Therefore, it's a good idea, when practicing your public speaking, to develop a few basic talks you give repeatedly, alternating them in the appropriate venues, if possible. Through the repetition, you master and memorize the material, which allows you to concentrate on the audience rather than your notes or visuals.

Not all of your practice, of course, takes place in front of a live audience. Given the limited opportunity to speak in front of people, you also have to spend a lot of time at home practicing in front of a mirror. Videotaping and watching your talks in the privacy of your own home is old—and sensible—advice. When you are actually speaking, you can't also be judging your performance. Seeing yourself on video is not always pleasant, but it is one of the quickest ways to spot and detect flaws and bad habits. Working with a speaking coach or giving a talk to an assembled audience of family or friends also has the benefit of getting you an informed and, one hopes, objective critique.

How many speeches and talks must you give to get better? Improvement in the beginning is rapid, because every time you speak, you gain confidence and experience. But speaking, like playing the piano or golfing, is a skill at which you can continue to improve throughout your lifetime.

Bestselling author Michael Masterson says that to become really competent at any skill, you have to do it for 1,000 hours. With coaching and study—taking courses, reading books, hiring a speaking coach—you may be able to cut that down to 500 to 800 hours. That sounds like a lot, but while it requires a significant commitment, it's far from unreasonable. If you practice speaking 10 hours a week, in one year you will have logged 500 hours, and in two years 1,000 hours. Professional speakers spend many years, even decades, perfecting their craft. Amateurs do what their schedule permits, but more practice is better than less practice.

Mainly, improving your presentation skills, and becoming a better speaker, comes down to a matter of attitude. If speaking well is important to

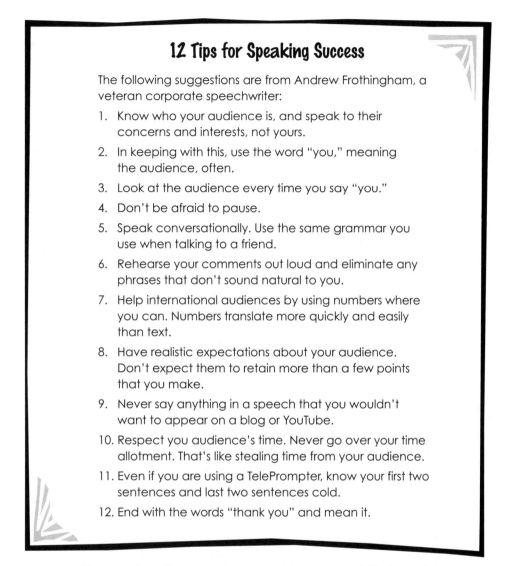

12 Tips for Speaking Success

The following suggestions are from Andrew Frothingham, a veteran corporate speechwriter:

1. Know who your audience is, and speak to their concerns and interests, not yours.
2. In keeping with this, use the word "you," meaning the audience, often.
3. Look at the audience every time you say "you."
4. Don't be afraid to pause.
5. Speak conversationally. Use the same grammar you use when talking to a friend.
6. Rehearse your comments out loud and eliminate any phrases that don't sound natural to you.
7. Help international audiences by using numbers where you can. Numbers translate more quickly and easily than text.
8. Have realistic expectations about your audience. Don't expect them to retain more than a few points that you make.
9. Never say anything in a speech that you wouldn't want to appear on a blog or YouTube.
10. Respect you audience's time. Never go over your time allotment. That's like stealing time from your audience.
11. Even if you are using a TelePrompter, know your first two sentences and last two sentences cold.
12. End with the words "thank you" and mean it.

you, you'll make the effort to improve and become a skilled, confident public speaker. If it's not important to you, you won't.

I'm guessing that, based on the fact that you bought or borrowed and read this book, there's something in your life that compels you to want to be a better public speaker. Perhaps you had a bad experience speaking in front of a group; it didn't go well, you were embarrassed, and you want to make sure that doesn't happen again. Or maybe you are a more-than-competent speaker, but you'd like to be even better.

Therefore, you more than likely already have the required attitude: a sincere desire to become a better, more persuasive, more interesting presenter of content-rich talks with genuine value to your audiences. In this book, I've given you tools and techniques for improving as a speaker that I've refined during my nearly three decades as a speaker, trainer, and seminar leader. As for the content, you either possess that already or can follow the guidelines I've laid out for researching content for your talks.

The only missing ingredient, then, is practice. You need to make the effort. Whether it's in front of the bathroom mirror at home or at the local Elks Club, you need to stand up and speak. The more you practice, the better you get, not only at delivering your materials but avoiding butterflies and gaining poise and confidence.

You get better at speaking by speaking and by listening to good speakers. Become a seminar/speech junkie. Attend public seminars on topics of interest by men and women with a reputation for being outstanding speakers. You may find certain things in their delivery you want to learn, copy, or adapt to your own presentations. And you may also find habits that irk you so much that you want to make sure you avoid them in your talks.

But be careful when going to hear a lot of speakers. The tendency is to copy and mimic speakers you like, and you don't want to take that too far. Remember, one of the things that sets you apart when you speak is your unique personality, background, experiences, and knowledge. The last thing the world needs is another clone of Motivational Speaker Model A with the tired clichés, the false drama, and the insincere manner. Honor your audience, and you, by being yourself, and giving your talk in your own way. After all, that's what they came to hear.

APPENDIX I
Sample Speeches

This speech, approximately 2,100 words, was written by speechwriter Charles Mizrahi and delivered by a mother with an autistic child. The goal of the breakfast meeting was to raise enough funds to start a school for autistic children in the community; one utilizing a new therapy that showed much promise. The school opened its doors a few months later with eight students, and planned to admit 20 new students later that year.

Good morning ladies, gentlemen, and very special friends,

Until three years ago, my life was very normal. My parents were average people who tried their best to raise seven children. My mother's parents, M— and M— S—, passed on to me and my siblings a love for the traditions of our great community. I attended community schools and at the age of 22, I was fortunate to meet a warm, caring, sensitive man, my husband D—. Four years ago, we were blessed with a daughter, M—, who was my pride and joy.

A little less than three years ago, on a rainy, cold April morning, we were once again blessed, this time with a son, A—. I recall the sparkle in my husband's eyes when he would hold A—. He was so proud and thankful that he now had a son who would one day sit next to him in synagogue, a son to play basketball with, a son who would one day stand proudly by his side as he accompanied him to the Torah as a bar-mitzvah.

My normal life began to end when A—turned one. From his first birthday on, I noticed something different about him. He was a very quiet baby and it seemed he was always in need of a nap.

Everyone told me how lucky I was to have such a "good" baby, one that didn't fuss and was not too much trouble, especially since I had my hands full with M—, only one year older. But my maternal instinct was telling me that something just wasn't right.

Over those several months, my concerns continued to grow. A— would sit for hours all by himself and play with strings; any type of string. Playing with strings now became his obsession. His next obsession was throwing anything not nailed down. Friends would comment on what a great pitching arm he had. All the while I continued to have a bad feeling that I just couldn't explain. A— also started to make strange guttural sounds that seemed far from normal. Everyone I confided in told me not to worry and that he would turn out just fine. To most of them I was just a nervous, neurotic mother. I wanted so much to believe them.

After some research, I called a psychologist for an evaluation. It was on a cool autumn day right before Thanksgiving that my life quickly changed. After extensive testing, A— was diagnosed with autism. It seemed like such a harsh diagnosis for such a small child. I did not cry, become enraged or even ask, "God, why me?" because I really didn't know what autism was. Sure, he did act a little different but there was no cause for a serious alarm. My beautiful dark-haired, brown-eyed A—, who had my smile, would now face a life full of challenges.

I began to research autism, to learn what it is and how my son could be helped. I learned that children with autism have a disorder that affects their interaction with the world. Autism impairs their social skills and their ability to use words to communicate with others. I found out that there is no "typical" autistic child. Autism is known as a "spectrum disorder," meaning there is a wide range of symptoms and various levels of severity. What all autistic children do share are deficits in social and language skills and different patterns of behavior. The more I researched, the more I was able to understand A—'s rather odd behavior.

It seemed the more I learned about autism, the more confused and scared I became. Over the past several years, I've been told that the number of children born with autism is reaching epidemic levels. One out of 166 children born today is affected with autism and boys have a four times greater chance of being born with autism than do girls.

As A— got older, my world changed in ways that prevent me from remembering what living a normal life was like. To say that my son is a handful is an understatement. Since children with autism have very little awareness of danger, I cannot rest or take my eyes off of him for even a second. I needed to remove the knobs from my oven because fire fascinated him and he had no fear of touching it.

A—'s throwing became worse. No longer a little boy, he would empty my bookshelves and throw books across the room. When he tired of that, he would start tossing plates, cups, utensils or anything within reach, with all his might.

When my husband went on business trips, I was petrified to be alone with him. I even slept with my air conditioner off, even in the heat of the summer, so I could hear if A— would get out of bed and move about the house.

Living with a child who has autism means being on call 24/7. My day usually starts at 5:30 AM, as A— barges into our room and jumps with all his might on our bed and on us. Children with autism have extremely high energy levels day and night. Imagine starting your day off with the energy level of a marathon runner who has just gulped down a gallon of coffee, and you get a glimpse of what life is like with A—.

Throughout the day, I am always at the ready should he start throwing a tantrum or put himself in harm's way. I look forward to his 7 P.M. bedtime. I must go through a whole sleeping ritual of holding his hand in a certain way, rubbing his back, until sleep finally overtakes him. Sometimes putting him to sleep can take minutes but many times it can be hours.

Once he is asleep, I collapse on my couch too exhausted to move. Finally I can rest, and to me this feels like a vacation—but it is bittersweet. I know that morning is in less than eight hours away, and the whole cycle will begin again. In a very short span of time, my life went from carefree and happy to constant stress and anxiety. Many times I feel like I'm running on a treadmill at high speed with no hope of it slowing down. I am not so concerned for my life but for my son's. The challenges my beautiful little boy faces each day are daunting. Simple things that one would take for granted, like communicating, going for a walk or eating a meal, are now hurdles that A— faces every waking hour.

Children with autism have a problem communicating; they live in their own world. They have trouble expressing themselves and no one knows why. It has to do with their neurological makeup and that's all we know. My heart aches and I have no more tears left to cry when I see how frustrated he gets when he wants something to eat and can't tell me.

Children with autism are very sensitive to the foods they will eat and A— likes only a handful of foods, such as avocados, hamburgers, eggs and bagels. I can't describe to you a mother's pain when she sees how frustrated her son gets and how he begins throwing plates, books, chairs, anything he can get his hands on—as hunger pains grip his small body. "Please, please, A—," I plead, "tell Mommy what you want to eat." I hold him and comfort him to no avail. This is just another cruel stumbling block that autism places between a mother and her child.

Children with autism have very little fear and do not recognize the dangers that surround them. Taking M— and A— out for a walk is a major ordeal. Since A— has no fear, his hand slips from my grasp and he dashes down the block before I can close the door. In just a flash, he can run from behind a car into the middle of the street. Carrying my daughter M— and running after A— have become a routine part of my day.

But by far the cruelest joke that autism plays on children and their mothers is its removal of something that for so long I took for granted. A— has never said he loves me. I want so much to be able to hold, cuddle, and kiss him, but many times he does not allow me. A soft kiss on the forehead one day will make him smile while that same kiss on another day will cause him to fly into a rage. It seems so unfair. All I want to do is give him love and get just a little back. But autism will not allow me that small comfort. A—'s wiring does not allow him to respond the way normal people do. I would give everything I have and then some to be able to hear him tell me that he loves me. I know that he does but I long to hear it from his lips. I pray that one day my prayers will be answered. And that day may not be so far off.

Today, a more effective form of therapy for children with autism is showing tremendous promise. Applied Behavioral Analysis, or ABA, is based on an early, aggressive, comprehensive intervention for children with autism. The recovery rate of children with autism has improved dramatically. In the past year, A— has been undergoing intense ABA therapy at home. The progress he has made over the past several months on home therapy is something I only dreamed about a short while ago. I am so thankful for small victories. Last week, he actually pointed to the apple juice and smiled when I poured him a cup. When A— was crying for something to eat the other morning, I offered him an avocado and he actually told me "No"; for A—, a major accomplishment. And he now allows me to gently kiss him on his forehead. I thank God for these small miracles.

I cannot begin to describe the progress A— makes when he has a strong ABA therapy day. He is proudest when he is able to identify things and communicate. Sadly after the age of three, A— no longer qualifies for home ABA therapy provided by New York State. Unfortunately, New York only provides early intervention up until the age of three. After that, we are left to fend for ourselves. It is our dream to have a school for our young children in the community where therapy can be continued. The Reach for the Stars Learning Center has come to our rescue.

Ladies and gentlemen, and dear friends: We need you to help us make this school a reality. Before my speech today, I was asked if I had made alternate plans for A—'s schooling if the necessary funds were not raised. To be quite honest with you, I did not even think about such a possibility because I do not allow failure to enter my mind. When a parent of an autistic child sees progress that only a short time ago would have seemed impossible, *failure is not an option!* I have the strongest faith and conviction that this school will be built because compassion is in every fiber of the Jewish soul. Our great community is known the world over for the acts of kindness it does. I have complete faith that our community will not let us down.

Let me close by sharing a dream that I play over and over in my mind each night, as A— lies quietly sleeping.

In my dream, it is Shabbat morning. The warm spring breeze feels so nice on my face, and as I walk out of our house, I can smell freshly cut grass. My husband is holding the hands of our daughters as they skip care-free along the sidewalk enjoying the beautiful spring morning.

I am walking slightly behind them, beside A—, my tall, handsome, strong A—. As we get to synagogue I take my seat in the front row of the ladies section. I beam with pride as A— is called to the Torah as a bar-mitzvah. After he reads from the Torah, he turns to find me. Our eyes meet and a smile lights up his face. He then mouths the words; "I love you Mommy," and my eyes overflow with tears of joy.

I firmly believe that this dream will one day become a reality... but only with your help. And for opening your hearts to children like A—, I pray that the Almighty will bless each and every one of you and your children, and your children's children with health, happiness and long life, AMEN.

The speech below, only about 1,500 words, was also written by Charles Mizrahi. It was delivered by a speaker at a breakfast meeting to launch a new organization (SAFE) to deal with drug, alcohol, and gambling addictions in his community. By the end of the speech, over $1.2 million was raised in less than 30 minutes.

Good morning ladies and gentlemen, and dear friends and family:

A few weeks ago on a warm summer day as I was sitting on my patio, I received a call from a SAFE member. He asked if I would share my memories on behalf of SAFE of my brother J—, who died at 20 years old from a drug overdose.

My first reflexive answer was NO, absolutely not. For so long now I have locked up some painful memories of J— in a small emotional closet in my mind. I rarely let anyone in. Some of those memories are so painful to remember let alone share. What good would come of it anyway? He persisted: "If you could make people aware about the dangers of addictive behavior and maybe, just maybe help one person, would you do it?" he asked. The question was hard and powerful and hit me in such a way that I had to share my thoughts with you today.

After reliving some memories that have not seen the light of day since J—'s death, I stand before you this morning.

So many nights I lie awake after my children and husband are sound a sleep and think about J—. A million "what ifs" race through my mind, perhaps things could have turned out differently. Maybe if we understood and paid closer attention to the warning signs he was giving us, events might have taken a better turn.

This morning I want you to hear about J— and what a great brother he was. His drug addictions that eventually lead to his overdose and death did not happen in a week a month or even a year. It took years of small little events and calls for help that were not fully answered.

As a little boy with two older sisters, J— was ours to take care of and love. J— was just a regular kid. He had happy and not so happy times just like the rest of us. His problems started when he didn't know how to deal with those not so happy times. You see, drug abusers were once innocent little boys, too.

The first call for help came when J— was in sixth grade and was asked to leave school. Although he was extremely bright and had a high IQ, he had a behavior problem probably the result of a learning disability. Today, he would have been placed in a special class and helped with his learning disability. But 25 years ago, he was stereotyped as a problem child. Seeing my mother's face after she hung up the phone with the school is an image I shall never forget.

Her face grew pale as she was told her J— would not be welcome back at school in the fall. She clasped her hand to her cheeks and seemed totally lost. J— was rejected with the title "failure" now hanging above his head.

So many times, more than I care to remember, I think about how all our lives would have been so different if SAFE was around. He might have been identified early on with a learning disability and have received help and attention. We could have been informed that children with learning disabilities have a higher risk of becoming alcoholics and drug abusers. In a more supportive environment, his friends might have been more caring and understanding. In my dreams, I see J— bike riding with me down Ocean Avenue, happy and carefree. But it was not meant to be.

The second call for help came on what should have been J—'s happiest day, his bar mitzvah. It was a beautiful spring day and I remember the smell of freshly cut grass in the air. I also recall the contrast of the big white limousine that was going to take us to the shul and how small and alone J— looked next to it. When we arrived at the reception, my sisters and I floated around like butterflies with our cousins and friends. My mother, looking like royalty, waltzed around the room as she greeted the guests. My father, who just retired from his business due to his declining health, seemed tired and frail as he sat having a cigarette with a few friends. And then there was J—. He didn't have many friends, and seemed lost and alone in the sea of people. His bar mitzvah was bittersweet, a happy day tinged with J—'s loneliness.

I wish I knew then what I know now. Children who feel isolated and alone withdraw so quickly that it becomes harder and harder to reach them. That is what was happening to J—. If SAFE was there, he would have taken classes in school taught by SAFE trained teachers on how to communicate better and build self esteem. His classmates would have learned peer sensitivity. Therapists trained in adolescent behavior might also have been able to deal with the problem better than we did. In my mind's eye I see J— sitting on my living room floor laughing as my children climb on his back. In my dreams, he is so happy and surrounded by people who love him.

The third and saddest warning came when J— was 15 years old. For all practical purposes, he was not in school and smoking pot became the focus of his day. Many times, he would he would wake up in the late afternoon, or sleep the day away. Although he was smart, charming and bright, his drug abuse caused mood swings and he couldn't hold down a steady job.

As time went by, it was getting more and more obvious that J—'s drug addiction was totally consuming him. Our family decided that he belonged in a drug rehab center. When the day finally arrived, I remember how grueling it was for all of us. When the time came to go, my little 15-year-old brother was scared, really scared. He bolted from the house as the car drove up, and raced down the block in order to get away. My cousin chased him down the street, and forcibly put J— in the car along with my mother and I.

Our ride to the rehab center had begun. Arriving at the center after a two and a half hour drive, J— was so scared he was crying uncontrollably. And on a crisp autumn day, we left J— him there weeping and alone. We kissed and hugged him and tried to make ourselves believe that everything would be all right.

Unfortunately, everything was not all right. After only two days, the drug rehab center called. J— wanted to leave and they had no power to hold him there. During the next four years, J—'s drug addiction went from terrible to worse. At the age of 20, when life should have been just beginning and the world a blank canvas for him to leave his mark on, J—'s life had ended.

If SAFE was with us then maybe J—'s rehab experience could have been different. We would have been assigned a captain from SAFE who would be with us every step of the way. A proper intervention would have been planned and maybe he might have gone to rehab more willingly. SAFE would have recommended a peer, someone with a similar problem to J—'s, to enter into rehab with. As peers, they would gain strength from one another, not be alone and might have a fighting chance. As I sit on my patio overlooking the ocean, I sometimes see J— lying on the sand, hands clasped behind his head, soaking up the hot rays of the sun. But unfortunately, it is only a dream.

Perhaps now you could understand my hesitation about sharing these memories with you. It has been difficult for me, very difficult. Today our community is blessed with a group of dedicated people who help families through the nightmare of addictive behavior. SAFE is going even further. They are going into the classroom to teach our children the dangers of addiction as well as build their self-esteem. SAFE is working to prevent addiction before it starts.

I know nothing I can say or do will ever bring my sweet, beautiful brother J— back to me. There will always be a hole in my heart and the hearts of all who knew and loved him. My prayer this morning is that each and every one of you open up your heart and commit to the success of SAFE. If sharing my memories with you today can prevent one family from the pain, hurt, anguish and loss that my family and I went through, I would consider my talk with you this morning a success.

Please help SAFE work to push back the forces of addictive behaviors that is now thriving in our community. And I am sure that you will join me in my prayer that the Almighty will comfort all those in pain, guide those who are lost, and to heal all those who are ailing.

AMEN.

Appendix II
Pre-Program Questionnaire

Whenever I am asked to speak anywhere, I give the meeting planner this form and ask him or her to fill it out and return it to me. It gives me a quick feel for several items I need to ensure a successful presentation. These include: the objectives and interests of the meeting planner (Questions #5, 8, 9, and 11); the type of people in the audience (Question #2); how much the attendees already know about the topic (Question #4); and what their attitude is toward having me talk to them about this subject (Question #3).

Pre-Program Questionnaire

This questionnaire is designed to help me tailor our seminar to the specific needs, interests, and background of the audience. Please answer each question as best you can and return this form to our office. Thanks!

1. Program you would like us to present for you:
   - ❑ Effective technical writing
   - ❑ Effective business writing
   - ❑ How to write copy that sells
   - ❑ How to use direct mail to generate more leads and sales
   - ❑ Selling your services
   - ❑ Successful selling
   - ❑ Keeping clients and customers satisfied
   - ❑ 14 ways to sell any product or service in a recession
   - ❑ Other: _____

2. Tell us a little more about the group.
   Number of people who will be in the audience: _____
   Average age: _____
   Male/female ratio: _____
   Annual personal income [if relevant]: _____
   Educational level: _____
   Average number of years with company or organization: _____
   Job titles/functions of people in the audience:
   1) _____
   2) _____
   3) _____

3. Which of the following best describes the attitude of the majority of your audience toward our upcoming training session?
   - ❑ Very eager and enthusiastic—really looking forward to it
   - ❑ Somewhat eager and enthusiastic, if perhaps a tad skeptical about our ability to deliver something they can use
   - ❑ Neutral: neither enthusiastic nor skeptical. Their attitude is "show me"

❏ Not terribly interested but not unhappy about going
❏ Hostile, bored, or both—don't want to go and are being forced
   to by supervisor or manager
❏ Smug—think they already "know it all"
❏ Other:_____

4. How well-educated is the audience in the topic of the seminar?
   ❏ They're all experts—the presentation should be advanced and on
      a high level.
   ❏ They're fairly knowledgeable but recognize there's always more to
      learn and room for improvement.
   ❏ They have some knowledge of the topic but haven't been
      exposed to it that much.
   ❏ They're novices and require a strong education in the fundamentals.
   ❏ Other:_____

5. What are the three most pressing challenges or problems faced by
   the members of your group?
   1) _____
   2) _____
   3) _____

6. Which professional speakers have you previously used to present
   programs on my topic?
   1) _____
   2) _____
   3) _____

7. Aside from #5 above, what are the three most significant events or
   trends to have occurred in your industry, or within your company or
   group, during the past year or so?
   1) _____
   2) _____
   3) _____

8. What are your specific objectives for our program (e.g.. what skills do you want your people to gain, what changes in attitude do you desire, what actions do you want them to take as a result of the training, etc.)?

1) _____

2) _____

3) _____

9. What specific information, strategies, techniques, or topics in particular do you want to make sure I cover in the program?

1) _____

2) _____

3) _____

10. Are there any issues or topics that you want me to avoid during the program?

1) _____

2) _____

3) _____

11. Have you any other suggestions or advice to help me make this program your best ever?

1) _____

2) _____

3) _____

Instructions: Please complete this form and mail it back to me at the address below:

Bob Bly, Seminar Leader/Consultant/Copywriter

22 E. Quackenbush Avenue

Dumont, NJ 07628

phone (201) 385-1220 • fax (201) 385-1138

APPENDIX III
Sample
Seminar Description

TITLE:

How to Write E-Mail Marketing Messages and Landing Pages That Sell

DESCRIPTION:

As a specialized information publisher, you have products to sell and an opt-in list of online subscribers to sell them to. Sending e-mail marketing messages to your e-list with a link to product landing pages is one of the most effective ways of increasing online sales and revenues. In this program, you will discover how to write compelling e-mail marketing messages and landing pages that increase clicks, conversions, orders, and profits—without causing your prospects to complain or unsubscribe.

WHAT YOU WILL LEARN:

- What works best in e-mail marketing today—long copy or short copy?

- A "paint-by-the-numbers" template for writing landing pages that increase your online sales.

- Lift your click-through rates (CTR) with "online freemiums" and "content sidebars."

- Find the right balance between content and sales pitch in your online marketing campaigns.

- Three types of subject lines that can increase click-through rates in your e-mail marketing campaigns.

- How to instantly establish credibility in your landing page copy and design.

- The seven most important factors affecting conversion rates in your landing pages.

- How to generate more orders by avoiding creativity in your e-mail marketing.

- And more....

ABOUT THE SPEAKER:

Bob Bly, a freelance copywriter specializing in direct marketing, has written for over 100 clients including Phillips, Boardroom, Agora, Medical Economics, Weiss Research, Brownstone, and KCI. He is the author of more than 70 books including *The Copywriter's Handbook* (Henry Holt). His websites are bly.com and thelandingpageguru.com. McGraw-Hill calls Bob Bly "America's top copywriter." He can be reached at 201-385-1220 or rwbly@bly.com.

APPENDIX IV
Attendee Audit Form

PLEASE COMPLETE AND RETURN THIS FORM.

1. Name _____ Title _____

   Company _____ Phone _____

2. Which of the following best describes the type of writing you do?

   ❏ business writing ❏ technical writing ❏ copywriting

   ❏ other:_____

3. Which of the following do you write as part of your job?

   ❏ ads   ❏ articles   ❏ brochures   ❏ catalogs
   ❏ direct mail   ❏ letters   ❏ manuals   ❏ memos
   ❏ proposals   ❏ reports   ❏ speeches
   ❏ white papers ❏ websites   ❏ online content ❏ e-mail
   ❏ others: _____

4. Please attach one or two short samples of your writing—1 to 2 pages each at most.

5. Which of the following writing problems do you have?
   - ❏ Deadline too tight
   - ❏ Copy is ruined in the approval process
   - ❏ Subject matter too technical for me to understand
   - ❏ Conducting effective interviews
   - ❏ Finding and using suitable graphics to go with my copy
   - ❏ Overuse of technical terms, buzzwords, and jargon
   - ❏ Overuse of clichés
   - ❏ Making spelling mistakes
   - ❏ Proper use of punctuation marks
   - ❏ Using correct grammar
   - ❏ Making complex subject matter clear and understandable
   - ❏ Making dull subject matter interesting to the reader
   - ❏ Expressing numbers and mathematical terms in writing
   - ❏ Overuse of abbreviations
   - ❏ Creating attention-getting headlines and subheads
   - ❏ Writing abstracts of longer pieces
   - ❏ Use of tenses
   - ❏ Keeping ideas in writing parallel
   - ❏ Overuse of antiquated phrases and stuffy language
   - ❏ Paragraphs and sentences too long
   - ❏ Words too big
   - ❏ Being concise and writing to fit the available space
   - ❏ Other: _____

6. What questions about writing do you have that you would like us to answer in the seminar for you?

   _____

   _____

   _____

7. What do you want to learn in this seminar?

    _____

    _____

    _____

8. On a scale of 1 to 10 (10 = superior, 5 = average, 1 = poor), how would you rate your writing skills: _____

9. What would it take to increase your rating of your writing skills to an 8, 9, or 10?

    _____

    _____

    _____

10. Any other requests, suggestions, or comments?

    _____

    _____

    _____

MAIL TO:
Bob Bly
CTC
22 E. Quackenbush Ave.
Dumont, NJ 07628
Fax to: (201) 385-1138
Call: (201) 385-1220

APPENDIX V
Audience Affinity Form

Find a different member of the group who has done each of these things or fits each of these categories:

Been to Disney World	Is married to someone taller than they are	Owns a boat	Plays a musical instrument	Attends church regularly
Has eaten sushi	Has a MySpace page	Swam with dolphins	Can do magic tricks	Has an advanced degree
A veteran of the U.S. Armed Forces	Has downloaded more than 500 songs onto their iPod	Likes to play basketball	Can bench press their own weight	Likes to watch videos on YouTube
Watches horror movies	Is an avid tennis player	Likes spicy foods	Has a cat	Likes to go fishing
Can run two miles	Knows how to drive a stick shift	Listens to rap music	Reads romance novels	Enjoys playing golf
Has three or more siblings	Is a Tom Cruise fan	Has three or more kids	Loves to play video games	Keeps an aquarium
Watches American Idol	Collects coins or stamps	Writes a blog	Speaks a foreign language	Has a dog

APPENDIX VI
Using Boolean Operators in Search Engines

Advanced search templates are a user-friendly presentation based on Boolean operators. However, in case such templates are unavailable, or a specific research requires modification of the parameters, you can use the Free-Form Boolean query, typing the commands onto the search bar. There are only three basic Boolean commands or "operators":

1. **AND:** finds only documents that contain all the search terms (can be more than two). Example: Query: I'm interested in finding all about albino elephants. Typing "albino" into Google's query bar on 4/10/07 resulted in 9,810,000 hits. "Elephant" awarded 34,500,000 hits. Typing "albino AND elephant" netted 369,000 hits (actually, Google no longer requires typing "AND"—it includes all search terms by default). Alternately, you can type a plus sign instead of the "AND": "albino +elephant". (Be sure to include a space between "albino" and the + sign, no space between the + sign and "elephant".)

2. **OR:** finds all the documents containing at least one of the words or phrases specified in the query. It also brings up all the documents that contain some or all the words. Query: I would like to find a CPA or an accountant. "CPA" typed into Google on 4/10/07 identified 34,500,000

results. "Accountant" gave 51,100,000, and "CPA OR Accountant" returned 66,600,000 results.

3. **NOT** (**AND NOT** on some of the search engines such as AltaVista): this operator excludes a word or a phrase from the results. Query: I want to learn about marsupials other than kangaroos. Typing "marsupials NOT kangaroo" into Google on 4/10/07 yielded 273,000 results, whereas "marsupials" and "kangaroo" separately brought in 1,150,000 and 13,300,000 hits respectively. A minus sign can replace the operator "NOT": "marsupials –kangaroo". (As with the plus sign, be sure to place a space between the "marsupials" and the –sign, no space between the –sign and "kangaroo".)

Use parentheses for commands that are combinations of the Boolean operators. Just like any other algebraic term, the parentheses tell the search engine to execute what's within them first. For example, for the query "I would like to learn about the intelligence of both gorillas and orangutans," type "intelligence AND (gorillas OR orangutans)". The search engine will attend to the "gorillas OR orangutans" first, then will add the "intelligence."

The *advanced search templates* offered by many of the search engines present a convenient way to use the Boolean logic in searches. The format for the advanced search is a query bar to be completed according to instructions (such as "with the exact phrase" or "without the words", etc.). Most search engines also offer one set of bars for Boolean search, and another for options such as choice of language, number of results per page, etc.

However, not all search engines have this feature, and even when they do it may not provide the best answer for the search. No matter—you can always use the Free Form Boolean search. Just type the operators onto the regular search bar according to their rules. Note—it is important to be familiar with the rules of each search engine, as they may change slightly from engine to engine ("slightly" should not be taken lightly—remember, computer programs may be very particular about the exact placement of a dot!).

Google's advanced search (google.com/advanced_search?hl=en) is similar to those of other search engines such as Yahoo. Additionally, it offers a useful cheat sheet for its operators. Some of these operators exist in the ready-made advanced search bars, and many others do not. Just type them in as needed.

Exalead (exalead.com/search) has a different approach in its advanced search. It combines the Free Form Boolean search and a ready-made menu into one. Rather than several bars, it has the regular search bar, and a list of options with instructions on how to use the operators. The options are divided into three categories—What, Where and When. "What" includes all the operators—exact phrases, forbidden terms, logical terms which include parentheses, etc. "Where" helps narrow the search by concentrating on certain geographical or World Wide Web locations. "When" includes time constrains pertaining to document modification dates.

There are other, more advanced operators or search commands you can use beyond "AND", "OR", "NOT".

- **NEAR**: a modification of the operator "**AND**". It is used to indicate proximity of the search terms, usually within 10 words—that is, when the terms relate to each other. For instance, this operator can be used to find a Sudoku in the shape of a jigsaw puzzle. If it isn't used, the search engine may bring up an article that talks about Sudoku in one paragraph and about jigsaw puzzle four paragraphs later—as two separate entities. The operator is used as "searchword1

NEAR searchword2". Google uses an asterisk for the "NEAR" command, where its format is "searchword1 * searchword2" (the asterisk may either have spaces on each side or not). For the example above the query is "jigsaw NEAR Sudoku" or "jigsaw * Sudoku" for Google. (The first hit, by the way, is the British site sudoku.org.uk/jigsaw.asp. It has a daily jigsaw-like Sudoku, with boxes of rather unusual shapes.)

■ **Synonym:** a squiggle sign (~) in front of the query tells the engine search to look also for synonyms. This command is recognized by most search engines. For example, the query "~auto" will bring the results for "car", "vehicle", "truck" etc. It's not clear if the MSN and Gigablast engines recognize this operator.

■ **Exact phrase:** the exact phrase is built into every advanced search feature. Additionally, all the search engines recognize brackets as exact phrase in their regular search bar. For example, the query "to kill a mockingbird" (typed with the quotation marks) will return only documents related to the Harper Lee's book including movies, DVD, discussions etc. Dashes between the words with no spaces (to-kill-a-mockingbird) is another form that expresses exact phrases and is recognized by all the search engines. Note: you can input more than one exact phrase in the query using this format.

■ **Site:** searches only within a certain site, an option offered by engines such as Google, Yahoo, AltaVista and Exalead. In Google the format is "searchword site:url" as in "statistics site:http://www.whitehouse.gov" —search for statistics in the White House site.

- **Date:** searches only within certain range of dates, a feature that exists in Google, AltaVista and Exalead. Google allows only a range of months, whereas Exalead allows searches for documents, which were modified before or after a specified date.

- **Link:** brings pages that contain links to a specified website, an option offered by Google, AltaVista, Gigablast and Exalead. Google's format: "link:url".

- **Filter of adult content** exists on Pagebull, AltheWeb, Yahoo and Google. Google uses the command "**safesearch**", e.g. "safesearch: sex education".

- **Domain:** finds all files with a specified domain in their name. On AltaVista, for example, the format is "domain:com" or "domain:uk".

- **Format:** allows a search of all files of the same type. For example, "filetype:pdf" on Exalead.

- **Info:** supplies information about a given page. For example, "info:url" on Google.

- **Range of numbers:** enables search within a range of dates or dollar values. For example, if you search on Google for a camera between $200 and $300, type "camera $200..$300" (two dots, no spaces).

- **Related pages:** finds websites related to the specified site. On Google, type "related:url".

- **Define**: brings up definitions for the terms in the query. Google's format is "define:searchterm".

APPENDIX VII
Resources

Books

DiResta, Diane. *Knockout Presentations: How to Deliver Your Message with Power, Punch, and Pizzazz* (Chandler House, 1998).

Howard, Vernon. Talking to an Audience (Four Star Books).

Kelley, Joseph J., Jr. *Speechwriting: The Master Touch* (Stackpole Books, 1980).

Pincus, Marilyn. *Boost Your Presentation I.Q.: Proven Techniques for Winning Presentations and Speeches* (McGraw-Hill, 2006).

Ridgeway, Bret. *View from the Back: 101 Tips for Event Promoters Who Want to Dramatically Increase Back-of-the-Room Sales* (Morgan James Publishing, 2007).

Smith, Terry C. *Making Successful Presentations* (John Wiley & Sons).

Theibert, Philip. *How to Give a Damn Good Speech* (Castle Books, 2005).

Zelazny, Gene. *Say It With Presentations: How to Design and Deliver Successful Presentations* (McGraw-Hill, 2000).

Periodicals

Executive Speaker, McMurry Publishing, McMurry Campus Center, 1010 E Missouri Ave, Phoenix, AZ 85014. 888-626-8779. (*For executives who wish to improve their speaking skills.*)

Sharing Ideas, Walters Speaker Services, PO Box 398, Glendora, CA 91740-0398. www.speakandgrowrich.com, 626-335-8069.

Magazines

Successful Meetings, www.successfulmeetings.com. (*Trade journal for professional meeting planners who hire speakers.*)

Vital Speeches of the Day, McMurry Publishing, McMurry Campus Center, 1010 E Missouri Ave, Phoenix, AZ 85014. 888-626-8779. (*Reprints the year's most important speeches and maintains an archive of more than 17,000 speeches.*)

Websites

jokesplace.com (*Free website loaded with jokes.*)

speaking-tips.com (*Free tips for businesspeople giving presentations and speeches.*)

quotationspage.com (*Free website compiling great quotations for speakers and writers.*)

Organizations

American Seminar Leaders Association, 2405 E. Washington Blvd., Pasadena, CA 91104. (800) 801-1886, www.alsa.com.

American Society of Training and Development, 1640 King Street, Box 1443, Alexandria, VA 22313-2043. (703) 683-8100, www.astd.org (*Association for professional trainers.*)

National Speakers Association, 1500 S. Priest Dr., Tempe, AZ 85281. (480) 968-2552, www.nsaspeaker.org. (*Association for professional speakers and aspiring speakers.*)

Toastmasters, International, PO Box 9052, Mission Viejo, CA 92690-9052. (949) 858-8255, www.toastmasters.org. (*Helps its members improve their public speaking skills at monthly local chapter meetings held throughout the U.S.*)

Glossary

BDF: a formula created by Michael Masterson for analyzing the core buying complex of the audience based on their beliefs, desires, and feelings. *Beliefs:* What does your audience believe? What is their attitude toward your product and the problems or issues it addresses? *Feelings:* How do they feel? Are they confident and brash? Nervous and fearful? What do they feel about the major issues in their lives, businesses or industries? *Desires:* What do they want? What are their goals? What change do they want in their lives that your product can help them achieve?

Blog: an abridgment of the term web log, a blog is an online diary or personal commentary.

Boolean logic: First discussed by the British-born, Irish mathematician George Boole (1815-1864), this is a method for formulating precise queries using true-false connectors or *operators* between concepts. This is a mathematical system which is used today for queries on the World Wide Web, and is designed to produce better search results.

Boot camp: an intensive workshop or seminar, usually held during two or three days, often during a weekend. Attendees pay to gain a skill or knowledge they believe can transform their lives; topics are wide ranging. Boot camps usually have multiple speakers, though often the promoter of the event is the main speaker.

Conference: an event ranging from one to three days in length, featuring multiple presenters, and typically aimed at either a business audience, hobbyists, or other affinity groups. Some speakers address the entire group; others make their presentations in *breakout sessions*.

e-Zine: an online magazine that caters to a niche or special interest subject matter. An online magazine may be online-only, or may be the online version of an otherwise print-published magazine.

Corporate training: classes held on site at a company to teach their employees skills useful in the workplace. Topics can range from soft skills such as time management and leadership to hard skills such as engine repair or data warehousing.

Demographics: the physical characteristics of a population, such as age, sex, marital status, family size, education, geographic location, and occupation.

Fly-in: a special effect (animation) transition found in PowerPoint.

Ghostwriter: a professional writer paid to write books, articles, stories, or reports that are officially credited to another person.

Hot buttons: major issues of concern to the majority of people in the presenter's audience.

Landing page: the page that website visitors arrive at after clicking on a link; generally a home page, or any other page in a site.

Lavaliere: a portable microphone hung around the neck of the user or clipped to a neck tie, shirt, or blouse.

LCD projector: A self-contained unit that combines LCD (liquid crystal display) panels and a high intensity light source for a complete computer and/or video projection device.

Leave-behind: an item given to audience members to take away from the presentation, such as a bound booklet containing copies of the visuals or a reprint of the speech,

Lectern: A stand that serves as a support for the notes or books of a speaker.

Mirroring: matching your tone, voice inflection, volume, vocabulary, speech patterns, and even accent to the people to whom you are speaking.

Niche: A situation or activity specially suited to a person's interests, abilities, or nature; a special area of demand for a product or service. Speaker Wally Bock defines a niche as the intersection of a topic (e.g., customer service) with an industry (e.g., banking).

Noise: non-consequential results.

Panel: a break-out session, usually an hour long, using shorter presentations by multiple panel members with a moderator/facilitator, rather than a presentation by a single speaker.

Pattern interruptions: a method of waking up an audience by introducing a change in their listening pattern; a productive interruption.

Podcast: an audio file, created in an MP3 format, that can be downloaded either to a computer or mobile device. Listeners can *subscribe* to audio file publishing services online to receive automatic downloads of serialized material.

Podium: a platform raised above the surrounding level to give prominence to the presenter standing on it.

PowerPoint: a presentation program developed by Microsoft, widely used by businesspeople, educators, students, and trainers.

Promotional seminar (or **product seminar**): a presentation designed ultimately to sell a product or service rather than be a profit center in itself.

Psychographic variables: attributes relating to personality, values, attitudes, interests, or lifestyles. They are also called IAO variables (for interests, attitudes, and opinions). They can be contrasted with demographic variables (such as age and gender), and behavioral variables (such as usage rate or loyalty).

SAP formula: *Subject*: the topic on which you speak; *Audience*: who you will be speaking to, including the demographics, education, background, and interest in your topic; and *Purpose*: the objective of the presentation—what you want to happen as a result of the attendees hearing your talk.

Seminars: public or private presentations given for educational purposes in a longer format—anywhere from two hours to several days, though most are a half or full day.

Speaking off the cuff: giving a speech given with little or no preparation; a presentation on a given topic where the speaker talks spontaneously, or "off the top of his head."

Tele-seminar: a seminar, speech, or other educational information delivered to a group on the phone via a shared conference line.

Three Ts Formula: A formula for creating a speech outline that states: Tell them what you're going to tell them. Tell them. And then tell them what you told them.

Tutorial: an informational seminar, with the pitch for the service limited to the beginning, the end, and the coffee breaks.

Webinar: a tele-seminar with a visual component added to the viewer's desktops via the internet; they are suited to situations where attendees can participate in their offices and have access to their own phone and PC.

Toastmasters: a national membership organization dedicated to helping people become better public speakers.

Workshop: a presentation involving attendee participation and interaction; the format of choice for skills that are best learned through hands-on experience and practice.

Citations

page 4   Ralph C. Smedley; Source:
          Goodman, Ted, *The Forbes Book of
          Business Quotations* (Black Dog &
          Leventhal, 1997)

Page 7   Source: Ogilvy, David, *Confessions
          of an Advertising Man*
          (Antheneum, 1963)

Page 10   Xanthes; Source: Dangennes, B.,
          Speech: How to Use It Effectively
          (Funk & Wagnalls, 1915)

Page 13   A.S. Gregg; Source: Goodman,
          Ted, *The Forbes Book of Business
          Quotations* (Black Dog &
          Leventhal, 1997)

Page 25   Source: Bradbury, Ray; *Zen and
          the Art of Writing (Bantam Books,
          1990)*

Page 26   Marcia Yudkin, professional
          speaker *(www.yudkin.com)*

Page 30   Ralph Waldo Emerson; Source:
          Goodman, Ted, *The Forbes Book of
          Business Quotations* (Black Dog &
          Leventhal, 1997)

Page 34   Source: Pincus, Marilyn, *Boost
          Your Presentation I.Q.* (McGraw-
          Hill, 2006)

page 43   Source: Sharpe, Alan, *Speak Like
          a Leader* (Andrew Spencer
          Publishing, 2008), p. 3.

Page 57   Xanthes; Source: Dangennes, B.,
          Speech: How to Use It Effectively
          (Funk & Wagnalls, 1915)

Page 59   Source: Howard, Vernon, *Talking
          to an Audience* (Sterling Publishing,
          1963)

Page 63   Richard Armstrong, speechwriter

Page 69   Source: Theibert, Philip, *How to
          Give a Damn Good Speech* (Castle
          Books, 2005)

Page 73   Isaac Asimov, writer

Page 74   Source: Ogilvy, David, *Confessions
          of an Advertising Man* (Antheneum,
          1963)

page 84   Source: Leeds, Dorothy,
          PowerSpeak Career Press, 2003

Page 88   Source: Kelley, Joseph,
          Speechwriting: the Master Touch
          (Stackpole, 1980)

Page 101 Source: Zelazny, Gene, *Say It With
          Presentations* (McGraw-Hill, 2000)

Citations

page 105   Source: Sharpe, Alan, *Speak Like a Leader* (Andrew Spencer Publishing, 2008)

Page 106   Ilise Benun, professional speaker

Page 128   Jonathan Swift; Source: Goodman, Ted, *The Forbes Book of Business Quotations* (Black Dog & Leventhal, 1997)

Page 133   Vanna White; Source: DiResta, Diane, *Knockout Presentations* (Chandler House, 1998)

Page 134   Parker, Robert, *Cold Service* (Penguin Books, 2005)

Page 136   Source: Theibert, Philip, *How to Give a Damn Good Speech* (Castle Books, 2005)

page 143   Source: Sharpe, Alan, *Speak Like a Leader* (Andrew Spencer Publishing, 2008)

Page 151   Source: Zelazny, Gene, *Say It With Presentations* (McGraw-Hill, 2000)

Page 152   Source: DiResta, Diane, *Knockout Presentations* (Chandler House, 1998)

Page 161   Source: Weiss, Alan, *Money Talks* (McGraw-Hill, 1998)

Page 162   Source: Howard, Vernon, *Talking to an Audience* (Sterling Publishing, 1963)

Page 168   Source: Ridgeway, Bret, *View from the Back* (Morgan James, 2007)

Page 172   Source: Kelley, Joseph J. Jr, *Speechwriting: the Master Touch* (Stackpole, 1980)

Page 173   Source: Weiss, Alan, *Money Talks* (McGraw-Hill, 1998)

Page 175   Spock, Dr. Benjamin, *Baby and Child Care* (Pocket Books, 1998)

Page 177   Source: Weiss, Alan, *Money Talks* (McGraw-Hill, 1998)

Page 184   Source: Ridgeway, Bret, *View from the Back* (Morgan James, 2007)

Page 188   Paul Hartunian, speaker

Page 198   Source: Kelley, Joseph, *Speechwriting: the Master Touch* (Stackpole, 1980)

About the Author

BOB BLY is a freelance copywriter, consultant, and seminar leader with more than 25 years of experience in business-to-business and direct marketing. McGraw-Hill calls Bob Bly "America's top copywriter." He has written speeches, presentations, ad copy, sales letters, and websites for over 100 clients including IBM, the Conference Board, PSE&G, AT&T, Ott-Lite Technology, Intuit, ExecuNet, Boardoom, Medical Economics, Grumman, RCA, ITT Fluid Technology, and Praxair.

Bob has given presentations to numerous organizations including: National Speakers Association, American Seminar Leaders Association, American Society for Training and Development, U.S. Army, American Society of Journalists and Authors, Society for Technical Communications, Learning Annex, Thoroughbred Software, Alliance Pharmaceutical, and New York University School of Continuing Education.

He is the author of more than 70 books including *Getting Started in Speaking, Training, and Seminar Consulting* (John Wiley & Sons) and *The Elements of Business Writing* (Alyn & Bacon). Bob's articles have appeared in *Cosmopolitan, Writer's Digest, Successful Meetings, Amtrak Express, Direct,* and many other publications.

Bob writes columns for *Early to Rise* and *Target Marketing*. The *Direct Response Letter*, Bob's monthly e-newsletter, has more than 60,000 subscribers.

His awards include a Gold Echo from the Direct Marketing Association, an IMMY from the Information Industry Association, two Southstar Awards, an American Corporate Identity Award of Excellence, the Standard of Excellence award from the Web Marketing Association, and AWAI's 2007 Copywriter of the Year. He is a member of the Specialized Information Publishers Association (SIPA) and the American Institute of Chemical Engineers (AICHE).

He can be reached at:

Bob Bly
Center for Technical Communication
22 E. Quackenbush Avenue
Dumont, NJ 07628
Phone: 201-385-1220
Fax: 201-385-1138
E-mail: rwbly@bly.com
Web: www.bly.com

Index

Index